THE

RAILWAY TRAVELLER'S HANDY BOOK

OF

Hints, Suggestions, and Advice,

BEFORE THE JOURNEY, ON THE JOURNEY,

AND

AFTER THE JOURNEY.

Published in Great Britain in 2012 by Old House books & maps,
Midland House, West Way, Botley, Oxford OX2 0PH, United Kingdom.
44-02 23rd Street, Suite 219, Long Island City, NY 11101, USA.
Website: www.oldhousebooks.co.uk
© 2012 Old House

A CIP catalogue record for this book is available from the British Library.

ISBN-13: 978 1 90840 234 9

Originally published in 1862 by Lockwood & Co., London.

Cover Image: 'Railway Undertaking', dated September 1852 and published
in *Punch, or the London Charivari*, volume XXIII.

Printed in China through Worldprint Ltd.
12 13 14 15 16   10 9 8 7 6 5 4 3 2 1

CONTENTS.

PAGE

A Few Preliminary Remarks 1

BEFORE THE JOURNEY.

Business Travellers	.	3	Conveyance to the Station	37
Pleasure-seekers	.	4	Arrival at the Station .	41
Health-seekers	.	5	Choice of Route .	43
Season-ticket Holders	.	8	Choice of Train .	45
Travellers in General	.	9	Railway Privileges .	47
Railway Guides	.	10	Railway Insurance .	49
Preparation for the Jour-			Choice of Class	52
ney—Packing, etc.	.	13	Choice of Carriage .	57
Travelling Equipage	.	17	Choice of Seat .	60
Fixing the Time of De-			Sending Females and Chil-	
parture	.	20	dren by Railway unac-	
Letters of Advice, etc.	.	22	companied .	61
Eve of Departure	.	23	Retaining Seat .	63
Be in Time	.	28	Procuring Ticket .	67
Travelling Costume	.	32	Signal for Starting .	70
Supply of Etceteras.	.	34		

ON THE JOURNEY.

Settling Down	.	72	Reading .	80
Stowing away Hand Lug-			Chess-playing and Card-	
gage	.	72	playing	82
Materials for Comfort—			Smoking .	83
Rug, Cap, and Cushion		73	Musing, etc.	83
Conversation .	.	75	Sleep	84

	PAGE		PAGE
Refreshment	86	Up Line and Down Line	98
Marking Carriage for Recognition	89	Railway Signals	99
Changing Carriages	90	Signalling Guard in Emergencies	101
Care of Railway Ticket	91	How to Act in Cases of Threatened Accidents	102
Looking-out for Station	91	Treatment of Railway Servants	105
Ventilation and Draughts	92	Economy in Companionship	107
Caution against Looking out of Window	93	Treatment of Unpleasant Travelling Companions	108
Caution against Standing by the Door	93	Bye-laws and Regulations	112
Caution in Passing through Tunnels	93	Peculiar Regulations and Characteristics of various Railways	115
Asking Information	94	Liability and Non-liability of Railway Companies	118
Branch Lines and Junctions	94		
Crossing the Rails	94		
Entering and Leaving Carriage while in Motion	97		

AFTER THE JOURNEY.

	PAGE		PAGE
Collecting Baggage	121	Forwarding Parcels by Company's Express	130
Meeting Friends	121	Noting time of Departure of Return Trains	130
Engaging Cab	122	Position of the Station	130
Disposal of Ladies and Children	123	Reaching across Country and Out-of-the-way Places	131
Looking after Luggage	124	Whiling away the time at the Stopping Stations	132
Reclaiming Lost Luggage	124	Rates of Telegrams	133
Sending Intimation of Safe Arrival	126	Accommodation for Railway Travellers	135
Despatching Telegraphic Messages	127	Excursion Guide	137
Hiring Porter	128		
Leaving Articles at the Station	128		

THE

RAILWAY TRAVELLER'S HANDY BOOK.

———◆———

A FEW PRELIMINARY REMARKS.

THE extension and ramification of railroads throughout the habitable globe, together with the daily
increase of railway traffic, are matters of notoriety.
Most persons undertake a journey at least once in
the course of the year, and it is no exaggeration to
state that every man, woman, and child may be ranked
as a railway traveller. Nay, more, there are those
who pass the greater part of their lives in a railway
carriage, flitting incessantly from one station to
another, and only breaking off their travels at night,
to resume them on the morrow. If, therefore, railway travelling be so general, and railway travellers
form so numerous a class, it may be reasonably an-
ticipated that a work touching upon the comforts and
discomforts, the conveniences and inconveniences of
locomotion, will meet with universal acceptance and
approval. Especially when it is considered how valuable is even one of these practical hints or suggestions,
of which some hundreds will be found in this little
volume.

In order to render the work more easy of reference, it is divided into three periods : BEFORE THE JOURNEY—ON THE JOURNEY—AFTER THE JOURNEY. This arrangement will admit of any special item of information being lighted on at once ; while the natural order which the various items take will render the manual a never-failing remembrancer and referee, from the moment the railway traveller conceives the idea of his journey until he has accomplished it.   At the outset of our task we are desirous of bespeaking the special attention of the various classes of railway travellers, by a few remarks which may prove individually applicable, and favourably dispose each class towards the objects of general interest which follow.

BEFORE THE JOURNEY.

BUSINESS TRAVELLERS.

COMMERCIAL travellers, and others who pass a great portion of their time on railways, would succeed in deriving much valuable information during their progress by dint of observation and inquiry. There are certain ins and outs of railway travelling which do not appear on the surface, but which are nevertheless intimately connected with its working. These matters, although of little moment to the occasional traveller, are worthy of being ascertained and treasured up by him whose movements in life may be said to be regulated by a railway time-table. It is impossible to define what we mean more intelligibly than by calling them *wrinkles*. For example, some one train may be more comfortable to travel by than the others : it may be less crowded, and carry a better class of company than ordinarily ; or the carriages and general accommodation may be of a superior kind. Innumerable hints of a similar nature may be gleaned, and chiefly by placing one's self in communication with station-masters, guards, porters, and others connected with the

line.   Through the same medium much local information may be obtained, which will serve as some sort
of guide to commercial operations.   For instance, a
traveller arrives at a place he has not hitherto visited,
he wishes to find out a certain class of traders in the
town, but he is totally ignorant of their names,
addresses, or extent of business.   The railway officials
connected with the station have probably resided in
the neighbourhood for many years, and in a few moments they could furnish every particular.   In doing
this they need betray no confidence, nor step aside
from the straight path of duty, while the alighting
passenger would be materially benefited by these few
minutes' colloquy.   There are numerous other suggestions tending to the economizing of time and money,
the avoiding of inconvenience, and the enhancing of
personal comfort.   These may be gained by the business traveller making up his mind not to miss a single
opportunity of inquiry and observation, and not to
be backward in reducing them to practice.

PLEASURE-SEEKERS.

We will suppose a person about to start on an
excursion, unpledged to any particular route, and
solicitous only of obtaining the greatest amount of
pleasure for his outlay.   In such cases, it would be
an excellent plan to collect the various excursion
schemes put forth by the railway companies.   To
compare the advantages offered one with the other,
to note the several stopping-places on the route, and
if these be not familiar, to glean, by aid of guide-book

or gazetteer, some knowledge of the places themselves, together with the objects of interest by which they are surrounded. Thus, the cost of the trip, and the privileges to be enjoyed, may be ascertained with something like reasonable certainty. With regard to pleasure seeking, it may be observed that each person has his peculiar notion of what pleasure is. Most of us plead guilty to a hobby, and nearly every man has a predilection for some sport, amusement, or pursuit, which he follows at every opportunity, and enjoys with greater zest than all others. The geologist with his hammer, the entomologist with his hand-net, the botanist with his microscope, the angler with his rod, and the sportsman with his gun—each presses forward with an ardour unaccountable to his neighbour, and in the prosecution of his particular enterprise finds an enjoyment which he would neither forego nor exchange. The opportunities for indulging in any special diversion will be found to favour particular localities. These facts are duly recorded in topographical works, may be readily referred to, and will thus put the pleasure-seeker in possession of a certain amount of capital to start with. In like manner the mere sight-seer may ferret out in what direction are to be found the largest store of curiosities and marvels, on which to feast his wondering eyes.

HEALTH-SEEKERS.

Lord Byron declared that the most exquisite of human enjoyments consisted in being borne swiftly through the air on horseback. Dr. Johnson, when being whisked along the highroad rapidly in a post-chaise, turned to his travelling companion, Boswell, and exclaimed with a jubilant air, " Sir, there are few things in life better than this !" Following up this theory of sensation, we are tempted to declare that the being whirled through space at the rate of thirty or forty miles an hour is most pleasurable in its effects.   To the over-wrought brain, or the over-strained mental faculties, to the toiler who has sunk into a state of exhaustion, this rapid locomotion acts as a most agreeable fillip.   Nor is this to be found alone in the journey itself ; the bustle of the station, the incidents of the platform and waiting-room, the chance chat in the railway carriage, all tend to arouse the faculties, and to impart to them a freshness which they lose in silent and persistent labour.

But there is a possibility of carrying this beyond due limits, as the following incident will show :—A gentleman in a delicate state of health was recommended by his physician to reside by the seaside. Having business in London which required his frequent attention, he determined upon selecting Brighton as his residence, so as to be within easy reach of the metropolis.   The South Coast Railway runs a train to and from Brighton and London—a distance of fifty miles—in an hour and a quarter.   Of this train the gentleman referred to arranged to avail himself twice a-week.   After a few days' sojourning at Brighton, his health became greatly improved.   On the first occasion of his going to town, however, he was seized with a violent headache, which grew worse as the day wore on, and which, after his journey down, left him in such a state of pain and prostration, that he was obliged to seek his bed immediately on his arrival at home. The next morning he had partially recovered, and in two or three days he regained his former improved condition of health. On his second visit to town, he was tormented with the same kind of violent headache, succeeded by an equal amount of prostration. Nature and the beneficent sea breezes once more revived him, when on the third occasion of a journey to London, he was attacked by precisely the same symptoms as on the two previous occasions. He now thought it time to make known these facts to his medical adviser, who was not slow in discovering the peculiar relation in this instance between cause and effect. The simple truth was, that the performance of a journey of a hundred miles within so short a space of time, and at such a rapid pace, had too greatly excited the nervous system, and had otherwise disturbed the functions of a delicate organization and a debilitated frame ; and the force of this conclusion was afterwards made apparent by a cessation of the headaches with a discontinuance of the journeys. To the jaded and toilworn, therefore, we would say, close your books, leave the desk, fly the study, hasten to the nearest railway station, and take a return ticket for some twelve or fifteen miles. On arriving at your destination, scud down the green lanes and across the fields, setting out at a brisk pace and maintaining it until your return to the departure station in a couple of hours' time. The journey homeward will appropriately cap the achievement; which, although we do not vaunt as a panacea for all the ills of life, we nevertheless declare, from experience, to be one of the very best repairers of health and restorers of spirits.

SEASON-TICKET HOLDERS.

When a person makes up his mind to reside at some place accessible by railway, there are several circumstances—supposing him to be a man of business and a frequent traveller—which it would be important for him to investigate. In the first place he should ascertain upon what terms a season-ticket can be procured, for virtually the railway fare is a part of the rent, and therefore ought to enter into the calculation of the probable cost when taking a house under these conditions. Secondly, he should learn the times of arrival and departure, so as to make sure that they are conformable both with his commercial and domestic arrangements. Next, he should glean whether the trains are habitually punctual or unpunctual. To a man of business the arrival of a train even a few minutes behind time is apt to prove of serious consequence. In most Government offices the *employés* are compelled to "sign on," as it is called, when they arrive in the morning; and as the hour strikes, a line is drawn across the book of entry, thus obliging all who come after to place their signatures below this line. By this simple arrangement the names of late comers can be gathered at a glance. When this occurs a few times only, and at distant intervals, it is usually visited with a fine or a mild reproof, but a frequent repetition of late arrival brings down upon the

head of the offender condign punishment, and sometimes results in dismissal. In ordinary employments,
this want of punctuality in commencing the duties of
the day is regarded as one of the worst traits in the
character of a man of business, and greatly tends to
shake the confidence of the employer. Even in cases
where a person is responsible only to himself, this
detention is always provocative of annoyance, and is
frequently attended with loss. Another consideration
is, the distance at which the place of business is
situated from one terminus, and the place of residence
from the other. For if the interval between these
two points is protracted, it follows that the getting to
one from the station will occupy more time than is
consumed by the journey itself. Nor is the distance
alone to be regarded; the means of conveyance should
be inquired into, both as regards the cost and the de-
pendence that can be placed upon them. Finally, it
would not be amiss to ascertain whether, upon extraordinary occasions, the company would be disposed to
accord the privilege of a special train, as when, for
instance, a party was made up to visit the theatre, or
other entertainment terminating after the time of
departure of the last ordinary train.

TRAVELLERS IN GENERAL.

But whatever be the motive which impels a person to undertake a journey, whether it be love, law,
business, pleasure, politics, or pelf, all render themselves for the time being amenable to the same regulations, subject to the same wants, and susceptible to

the same ameliorations. Glancing at these in their
natural order, and assuming the intending traveller to
be sitting in his room a day or two previous to his
departure, turning his future movements over in his
mind, the first things which will commend themselves to his attention are those useful publications
known as

RAILWAY GUIDES.

Of these, there are two in common use—the
A B C and *Bradshaw*. Both are published on the
first of each month, and both contain the latest alterations in the fares, times, etc., up to the moment of
going to press. Generally speaking, these alterations
are not material, and the guide for one month might
in the majority of cases be made to do duty for another. Still the possibility exists of a change having
been made; to be prepared for which it is as well to
possess the publication of the current month. And,
by the by, when the purchase is made, the date on the
cover should be referred to, in order that a guide of
the time past may not be bought in mistake for one
of the time present. The *A B C Railway Guide* is,
as its title imports, a work easy of reference, the names
of the places being alphabetically arranged, and the
times of departure and arrival, the fares, etc., being so
clearly given as to prevent the possibility of a mistake.
It is, however, chiefly adapted for the use of persons
who have only to proceed direct from one point to
another, without being doomed to thread the labyrinth
of branch lines, junctions, etc. *Bradshaw*—the well-
known *Bradshaw*—is the other guide taken into the

railway traveller's confidence. This work contains a mass of information compressed into the very smallest compass, but on that account, and by reason of various signs and symbols having to be made use of, it is not so easy of interpretation as it might be. This fact has given rise to innumerable witticisms on its unintelligibility. And we must confess, that although we are acquainted with a few of the initiated to whom Bradshaw is as easy as A B C, we have never yet met with a lady who did not regard it as a literary puzzle, while the majority of the sterner sex have failed to master its intricacies. Knowing by experience the great value of this *vade mecum*, and desirous that others may equally appreciate it, we will endeavour to furnish a key to some of the most prominent difficulties, in a few brief suggestions which may be collectively termed "How to read Bradshaw." 1. When you are searching for the name of a place, refer to the alphabetical index at the commencement of the guide, and you will be directed to the appropriate page. 2. To ascertain the time of departure from, or arrival at, any place, run your eye along the figures which cross the page in a line with the name of the station. 3. When a train passes a station without stopping, it is indicated by two dots, thus •• 4. When a train stops at some given point without proceeding further, it is notified by a thick black line ▬, or by the word "Stop." If any train be shown below in the same column, it is an independent one. 5. The course of the main line is denoted by thick marks down the right hand side of the station columns; deviations or branches are indicated by thin lines. 6. A thin line in the middle of trains, thus ⌣, represents a shunt, and is intended to show the continuous route of the traveller. 7. Wave lines, thus ᨳ, have a twofold use; first, to direct the eye into the next train, and, second, to show that passengers do not travel past the stations opposite to which the wave line appears. 8. The various letters, as *a*, *b*, *c*, etc., occasionally met with in the tables usually refer to explanatory notes at the foot of the page. 9. Through routes, steamboat, omnibus, and coach communication in connection with the trains, will be found towards the end of the guide, after the tables of the ordinary lines. Finally, beware of mistaking the up-trains for the down-trains, or *vice versâ*. Be quite certain that you have learnt the proper time of arrival or departure, and refer a second time to prevent the possibility of error. Ascertain beyond doubt that the train you intend going by stops at the station for which you are bound; all sorts of exceptional cases are mixed up with many intermediate stations, and the ordinary routine is departed from in reference to market-days, and other local exigencies. Much valuable information respecting hotels, boarding-houses, apartments, etc., in the various towns in the United Kingdom, will be found scattered through the latter portion of the guide. The glowing terms in which nearly every proprietor speaks of his establishment must not, of course, be interpreted literally. Nevertheless it is something to ascertain the names and whereabouts of these temporary homesteads; and and in these days of extortion and anti-extortion such notifications as the following are worthy of being treasured in the memory; for example, " No charge for candles at this hotel." "A fixed charge for attendance." "A list of refreshments exhibited in the coffee-room." "Visitors are not expected to take wine," etc. etc.

PREPARATION FOR THE JOURNEY.—PACKING, ETC.

Most persons appear to have an instinctive horror of "packing-up." Some are happily in a position to depute the business to others, but by nearly all the process is avoided until the very last moment. The consequence is, that things are hastily thrown together pell-mell, without any attempt at order or arrangement; dresses are rumpled, coats are creased, linen soiled, rough articles are brought into unseemly contact with the delicate, the dirty associated with the clean, to say nothing of tricklings of ink, and streams of oil, which are apt to escape from their ill-secured receptacles. Our first piece of advice is, that railway travellers should confine their luggage within as narrow limits as possible, not encumbering themselves with a number of useless articles, or with such as may be obtained at the point of destination as readily as at home; to take, in point of fact, only the necessary and the indispensable. The Romans gave the name of *impedimenta* to their baggage—a word which pretty clearly interprets both ancient and modern opinion. The gallant General Sir Charles Napier declared that the only equipment required by an Indian officer comprised a second shirt, two pairs of socks, and a tooth-brush. But although few would be inclined to subscribe to the latter scanty outfit,

there cannot be a doubt that the traveller who is able
to carry his luggage in his hand is a comparatively free
man, while he who has many packages to look after
is, for the time being, a slave. It should be also
borne in mind that extra luggage entails extra expense; every trunk, portmanteau, or bandbox, carries
with it a certain charge, and can scarcely be touched
by the tips of strange fingers without having an im-
post levied upon it. There are numerous instances,
however, where large quantities of luggage cannot be
escaped. In such cases it would be advisable to adopt
the following course: Classify the articles in such a
manner that the same sorts shall have separate boxes
or distinct places assigned them. Thus, pack all the
heavy articles by themselves, or dispose them in the
bottoms of the boxes, etc. Place all the articles not
required for immediate use by themselves, and those
that are so required by themselves. Carry the articles
which you will need when you reach your journey's
end, such as night-dress, brushes and combs, etc., in a
travelling-bag, so that you may be spared the pain
and labour of uncording and unpacking at a moment
when it goes sorely against the grain. Attach to the
inner side of the lid of each package a list of the
various articles which such package contains; then
number each package, and finally make a memorandum
of these lots, with their corresponding numbers, in
your pocket-book, so that when at any time you
require a particular article, you can, by referring, at
once determine where such article is to be found. If
you are solicitous about the exterior of your luggage,
envelop it in canvas, the pulling and hauling, the

pitching and tossing, the friction and jostling, which packages are subjected to in travel, to say nothing of the paste-brush which the railway porter impartially applies to the effects of patrician and plebeian, are not calculated to improve the appearance of polish or paint. When packages are corded, they should be corded tightly and securely; in such cases, the cordage is regarded as the legitimate medium for lifting and carrying; therefore, if it be loose, or the knot insecurely fastened, prepare yourself to see your package lying smashed on the ground, its contents strewn in every direction, and the porter gazing at you with the cord in his hand, and a reproachful look on his features, for having supplied him with so treacherous a holding. The directing of luggage is a matter of no small importance, carelessness in this particular frequently causing the miscarriage of packages. The name and address should be written legibly, and in a bold hand. Observe, also, that the name of the place should be in larger letters than the name of the person; and however much this may offend our self-esteem, it must be borne in mind that in the hurry and bustle of departure, the destination is what is first required to be known, the owner being a secondary consideration. When address labels are attached by tying, they should be of leather, parchment, or some such untearable material. One may frequently note a strip of writing paper, with the superscription traced on it in microscopic characters, the said strip partially strangled with twine or thread, and tenderly attached to the handle of a package; an arrangement that may answer the purpose of indicating the birth-place of

the embryo lupine in a garden plot, but ill adapted for
the rough usage of the railway station and the exigencies of the luggage van.   Cards of address, fastened
on by tacks, are not to be recommended, for the cards
are apt to be torn away by contact with other packages, leaving the tacks standing alone as monuments
to the memory of the departed.   The best plan is to
paste the labels on to the luggage, as they will thus
more certainly retain their position ; for this purpose
adhesive labels are prepared and sold, which have only
to be wetted and applied in the same way as postage
stamps.   To avoid confusion, and to prevent things
being mis-sent, it is advisable to remove the labels
having reference to previous journeys.   As a crown-
ing precaution, it would be as well to place the name
and destination of the owner of the luggage *inside* as
well as outside, so that in the event of the latter being
destroyed, a clue to the claimant may be furnished.
The number of articles which are constantly travelling
out of their legitimate course, through carelessness in
the matter of address, exceed belief.   Some curious
stories could be told of railway travellers and their
luggage chasing each other half over the United Kingdom ; by some unhappy mischance, never happening
to reach the same place together ; so that the "*Adven-
tures of Japhet in Search of his Father*," or "*Cœlebs in
Search of a Wife*," are but tame and uninteresting
narratives compared with "Tomkins in Quest of his
Trunk."

TRAVELLING EQUIPAGE.

There are, perhaps, few things upon which human ingenuity has been brought to bear with such force as travelling conveniences. The distant traveller and the tourist, the family man and the bachelor, he whose means and desires are unlimited, and he whose resources are circumscribed, and whose requirements are few, has each been considered.

Many of us can remember the clumsy and cumbrous trunks and boxes of a bygone period, rendered clumsier and heavier still by outworks of brass-headed nails and bands of iron. Also those extraordinary carpet-bags, in which nothing could lie flat, and from which everything emerged in a dreadfully dilapidated state. *Mais nous avons changé tout cela*, and now travelling trunks, portmanteaus, bags, etc., may be had in every conceivable variety of make, shape, and size. For family purposes, a species of large trunk has been invented, which, when its outer covering is removed, resembles a chest of drawers, partaking, indeed, of all the convenience of that well-known article of household furniture without its cumbrousness. Trunks there are, also, of a smaller size, divided into compartments, affording facilities for arranging the wardrobe, and for separately placing away each article of dress. Of portmanteaus there exist a great variety, some on a large scale, and substantially made, so as to approach nearly the genus trunk, others with collapsing propensities, enabling the capacity of the receptacle to be considerably extended when occasion requires, and materially diminishing the bulk when not in use, by which means it becomes a large or a small portmanteau according to the contents. Another portmanteau is made of a size to admit of its being placed under the railway seat, and has the handle placed in such a manner that it may be easily carried by the owner. An equal amount of ingenuity has been displayed in connection with travelling bags. There is one of a hybrid nature, being a travelling bag upwards and a portmanteau downwards, proving as convenient as the latter, and as portable as the former. Another kind of bag is made to open square, enabling the articles to be placed in on a firm basis, and not coaxed or jammed in sideways, as in the ordinary bag.

As travelling bags are put into requisition more generally than any other kind of travelling gear, it will not be amiss to describe a bag recently introduced, which is made to contain the various toilet requisites, as well as articles of attire, and which possesses the combined advantages of compactness and portability. This bag is constructed to open in such a manner as to present the whole of the fittings standing erect in the centre, leaving the sides free. By a simple contrivance it is further made to open at the bottom. On two boards or standards are displayed the fittings; the boards, being supplied with a long hinge and handle, may be lifted out of the bag, and made to stand firmly on a table; the sides then lying flat, are in a convenient position for packing. The inner parts of the sides are provided with strong flaps, and also strong elastics and fasteners, to confine any article packed under them. One side of the bag can be opened to the bottom, leaving the other side still upright. The bag can be used without the fittings, the whole interior being then available for packing besides the flaps. It is also supplied with a new form of handle, the ends of which slide in grooves, thereby allowing it to lie quite flat on the top of the frame.

From bags we come to a species of knapsack, which is generally strapped on to the back, but being fitted with a handle on the top it may, when not used as a knapsack, form a convenient substitute for a travelling bag. Haversacks and wallets come next in order, these are made to contain a change of linen, toilet requisites, etc., and are slung across the shoulder by a strap. For persons who are going short journeys, or who intend to pedestrianize, this is, perhaps, the best kind of travelling appendage that can be conceived; it renders its wearer at once independent and easy. He can go from place to place without being importuned by touts and tag-rag. He enters an inn, and leaves it without any of that parade or sensation which even the smallest of travelling bags appears to engender, and he can always have whatever he requires ready at hand, and soon becomes so accustomed to his general burden, as to be scarcely aware that he is carrying anything at all. Dressing-cases are designed of every form and variety, and in keeping with the utilitarian spirit of the age, are also made to combine with the customary portmanteau or travelling bag, the articles being so disposed as to fill up vacancies which would otherwise remain unappropriated. Another convenient form of dressing-case is that where the toilet requisites are spread, if we may so term it, on a strip of leather, and are then

capable of being rolled up into a small compass.   Nor
have ladies been forgotten in the matter of travelling
equipages.   There are ladies' wardrobes, ladies' portmanteaus, ladies' compendiums, ladies' bonnet trunks,
etc., each admirably adapted for the various purposes
to which it will be put.   The travelling receptacles
chosen, and the luggage packed, the next consideration is—

FIXING THE TIME OF DEPARTURE.

In answer to the question whether it is better to
travel by day or by night, we should say that much
depends on the constitution and temperament of the
traveller.   It is decidedly imprudent for a delicate
person to expose himself to the night air, which to
some extent he must do, however securely the doors
and windows of the carriage may be closed.   Nor can
the deprivation of the usual night's rest be conducive to
health.   For although, in some exceptional cases, there
are travellers who can sleep as soundly on the railroad
as in their beds, the majority of travellers, in spite of
every effort, fail on procuring any slumber beyond
that homeopathic amount familiarly known as " forty
winks."   But setting aside the drawback of broken
rest, some persons maintain that there are certain
recommendations which render night travelling preferable to travelling by day , one is, that people are,
generally speaking, more sociable, the darkness and
stillness of night appear to dispel that distrust and
snyness with which English travellers habitually regard each other by day, so that the journey is made

agreeable by conversation and the interchange of courtesies. To the very timid, another recommendation is that there is less chance of collision, the line being comparatively clear, and extra precaution being taken to prevent the possibility of accident. Some persons prefer starting by the last train at night to the first train in the morning, because the excitement attendant on the journey, and the dread of oversleeping themselves, entirely breaks up their night's rest, and renders them in a very unfit state to set out upon their travels. If the day be chosen, the hour of departure should be regulated, to some extent, by the time of arrival. It is very awkward, for instance, to invade the domicile of a country friend in the middle of the night, and owing to the absence of suitable arrangements it may prove equally unpleasant to the invader. In cases where the traveller is bound for some across country place, and has to depend upon a public conveyance to transport him to his final destination, he should assure himself that the omnibus, coach, or fly, will be at the station to meet the train he travels by ; and on extraordinary occasions he may secure the attendance of a conveyance by a polite request, either by post or telegraph, being forwarded to the superintendent of the station at which he intends to alight.*

---

* This puts us in mind of a certain incident which occurred to us in one of our journeys. We arrived at dusk at a little sequestered station, and determined upon walking to our place of destination. Shortly after we set out, however, the darkness of night came on suddenly, and we thought we should now rather prefer riding. Just at that moment we met " a weary ploughman plodding his homeward way;" we hailed with " I say, my

LETTERS OF ADVICE, ETC.

When the traveller is about to visit an hotel or
lodging-house, he will insure a comfortable reception
by writing a letter, a few days prior to his departure,
to the proprietor of the house he intends staying at,
instructing him to prepare certain rooms, and make
such other arrangements as may be necessary, it would
be as well if the letter were posted in sufficient
time for an answer to be received before the day of
starting, so that the traveller may be assured of his
arrangements being carried out, or in the event of it
being impossible to comply with his request, that he
may be made acquainted with the fact. Even when
the visit is about to be paid to a friend, where there
is always a welcome, the proposed visit should be
notified, to save inconvenience to all parties. There are
very few people who like to be taken by surprise, and
the usual exclamation of, " If I had only known that
you had been coming," is sufficiently indicative of the
disappointment felt. Should you require a ladies'
carriage, a horse-box, or a carriage-truck, write to the
station-master a day or two previously, as they are
not always to be had at the moment. In cases of
invalids, or decrepit persons, it would also be as well

man, we want to go to ———, can you tell us if there are any
vehicles about here." To which he replied, " I don't know
nothink about wehicles, but there's a great big pond in the next
field, and if you don't look out you'll tumble into it." *Moral.*—
A traveller arriving late at an out-of-the-way place, without any
previous arrangement or intimation, is more likely to find ponds
than " wehicles" to receive him.

to write to the station-master, or other authority, beforehand, to endeavour to secure such conveniences and comforts most favourable to the sufferer's infirmities. At the same time it should be borne in mind, that although there is every disposition on the part of the different railway companies to be as considerate as possible, still they cannot be expected to confer special advantages on individuals, to the detriment of the public interest and the general working of the establishment.

EVE OF DEPARTURE.

We have now arrived at a period within a few hours of starting on the intended journey, say the night before. At this juncture the traveller, like a wary general, reviews his forces, and places his baggage in order, ascertaining that the addresses are all properly affixed, the locks secured, and the straps and cords fastened. If the intention be to start very early in the morning, a vehicle should be engaged overnight, and the driver instructed to be at the door in ample time for the removal of the luggage and the getting to the station. But by the time the vehicle arrives, you yourself should be ready to step into it. To this end, it will be necessary to ask a policeman, or some person whose duty takes him abroad at night, to call you at the proper hour. In some country towns the people who have to attend the markets are in the habit of chalking opposite to their doors overnight, the hour at which they wish to be aroused the next morning. Thus the policeman reads his instructions as he walks his beat, and awakens the inmates accordingly. This hint might be acted upon by railway travellers; for the person who had been spoken to, might forget the number of the house, the hour at which he was to call, or possibly lose sight of the circumstance altogether, unless thus reminded. Again, some persons sleep so soundly that the noise of the door-bell or knocker fails to impress their auditory nerves. In many of the manufacturing districts of England, the factory hands employ a watchman, who is paid by subscription, and whose especial duty it is to arouse at certain hours those by whom he is employed. For this purpose he is armed with a long cane or wand, and the habitations of the factory people being for the most part low built, he is enabled to tap at the bedroom windows, and this he does in every case until he receives a response from within. It is well known that no sound from without sooner startles a sleeping person than a noise against the window. Acting upon this hint, the person who arouses the railway traveller might discharge against the window of his bedchamber a little gravel, or a few small shot, following this up by a vigorous ring of the bell; the one sound effectually breaking in upon slumber, and the other acting as a reminder.

But the best plan of all to insure being in time for an early train, is to sleep the night previously at an hotel adjoining, or adjacent to, the departure station. Here there will be little fear of awakening as the bustle in the passages and various bedrooms of other early travellers will, generally speaking, be suf-

ficient to awaken the heaviest sleeper. To avoid, however, the possibility of miscarriage, order the "boots"
to call you at the required time in the morning.

It happens, in numerous instances, that virtuous
resolves are made overnight with respect to early
rising, which resolves, when put to the test, are
doomed only to be broken. Some years ago a clergyman, who had occasion to visit the West of England
on very important business, took up his quarters, late
at night, at a certain hotel adjacent to a railway, with
a view of starting by the early train on the following
morning. Previous to retiring to rest, he called the
"boots" to him, told him that he wished to be called
for the early train, and said that it was of the utmost
importance that he should not oversleep himself. The
reverend gentleman at the same time confessed that
he was a very heavy sleeper, and as there would be
probably the greatest difficulty in awakening him, he
(the "boots") was to resort to any means he thought
proper in order to effect his object. And, further,
that if the business were effectually accomplished, the
fee should be a liberal one. The preliminaries being
thus settled, the clergyman sought his couch, and
"boots" left the room with the air of a determined man.
At a quarter to five on the following morning, "boots"
walked straight to "No. Twenty-three," and commenced a vigorous rattling and hammering at the
door, but the only answer he received was "All
right!" uttered in a very faint and drowsy tone.
Five minutes later, "boots" approached the door,
placed his ear at the keyhole, and detecting no other
sound than a most unearthly snore, he uncere-

moniously entered the room, and laying his brawny hands upon the prostrate form of the sleeper, shook him violently and long. This attack was replied to by a testy observation that he "knew all about it, and there was not the least occasion to shake one so." "Boots" thereupon left the room, but somewhat doubtingly, and only to return a few minutes afterwards and find the Rev. Mr. —— as sound asleep as ever. This time the clothes were stripped off, and a species of baptismal process was adopted, familiarly known as "cold pig." At this assault the enraged gentleman sat bolt upright in bed, and with much other bitter remark, denounced "boots" as a barbarous fellow. An explanation was then come to, and the drowsy man professed he understood it all, and was *about* to arise. But the gentleman who officiated at the —— hotel, having had some experience in these matters, placed no reliance upon the promise he had just received, and shortly visited "No. Twenty-three" again. There he found that the occupant certainly had got up, but it was only to replace the bed-clothes and to lie down again. "Boots" now felt convinced that this was one of those cases which required prompt and vigorous handling, and without more ado, therefore, he again stripped off the upper clothing, and seizing hold of the under sheet, he dragged its depository bodily from off the bed. The sleeping man, sensible of the unusual motion, and dreamily beholding a stalwart form bent over him, became impressed with the idea that a personal attack was being made upon him, probably with a view to robbery and murder. Under this conviction, he, in his descent, grasped "boots" firmly by the throat, the result being that both bodies thus came to the floor with a crash. Here the two rolled about for some seconds in all the agonies of a death-struggle, until the unwonted noise and the cries of the assailants brought several persons from all parts of the hotel, and they, seeing two men rolling frantically about in each other's arms, and with the hand of each grasping the other's throat, rushed in and separated them. An explanation was of course soon given. The son of the church was effectually awakened, he rewarded the "boots," and went off by the train.

Fortune subsequently smiled upon "boots," and in the course of time he became proprietor of a first-rate hotel. In the interval the Rev. Mr. —— had risen from a humble curate to the grade of a dean. Having occasion to visit the town of ——, he put up at the house of the ex-boots. The two men saw and recognized each other, and the affair of the early train reverted to the memory of both. "It was a most fortunate circumstance," said the dean, "that I did not oversleep myself on that morning, for from the memorable journey that followed, I date my advancement in the Church. But," he continued, with an expression that betokened some tender recollection, "if I ever should require you to wake me for an early train again, would you mind placing a mattress or feather-bed on the floor?"

BE IN TIME.

This will not be an inappropriate place to impress upon the railway traveller the importance of punctuality. The old adage of "Time and tide wait for no man" may be applied in this direction, only for the word tide read "trains." The time of departure stated in the table is no fiction; the strictest regularity is observed, and indeed must necessarily be, to prevent the terrible consequences that might otherwise ensue. Therefore passengers, to insure being booked, should be at the station five minutes earlier than the advertised time of departure. The doors of the booking-office are usually closed at the time fixed for the departure of the train, after which no person can be admitted. It should here be observed that the clocks at the various railway stations are universally set and regulated by "London time." For instance, most of our readers are aware that when it is twelve o'clock in the metropolis, it is either earlier or later than that hour elsewhere, according to the distance from London, and the direction of the compass. Thus the clocks of a provincial town may point at five minutes to twelve, whereas it has already struck twelve in London, and the train appointed for departure at that hour has started, when the unmindful traveller thinks that he has still a few minutes to spare. Bearing this fact in mind, it will be wise, upon alighting at a provincial station, to note the difference between the time registered there and the London time, so that the discrepancy may be duly allowed for in the traveller's subsequent movements. Beware of placing too great a reliance upon the domestic clock; these are generally eccentric in their movements, and by some sort of fatality, when most relied on, most mislead. The reason why persons are late for the train, generally arises from an overweening confidence in there being " plenty of time;" the interval between starting for the station and arriving at it is too finely calculated, or too short a time is allowed for the performance of certain things.

We hope that we shall not be accused of a want of gallantry when we declare that when there are ladies in the case, it is absolutely necessary to allow a wider margin for the preparations for departure than is ordinarily assigned. The fair sex *must* complete their toilet to their entire satisfaction, whatever the consequences may be. It should also be remembered that they do not enter into the spirit of the straight-laced punctuality observed by the railway authorities, and if the time-table sets down the departure at 1.20, they instinctively read 1.45. In such cases, it is absolutely necessary to adopt some stratagem to insure being in time for the train; the precise *modus operandi* is left to the ingenuity of the traveller, and the opportunities that may present themselves.

Perhaps the following anecdote may furnish a hint on this head:—A gentleman, engaged in commerce, had for a wife a lady possessed of every charm and nearly every virtue; there was one defect in her composition, however, which negatived many of her good qualities, and went far to disturb the domestic bliss which should have otherwise reigned—namely, an

utter disregard of punctuality in the regulation of her
domestic duties.   Many were the cold looks, the
harsh rebukes, the bitter rejoinders, and the sulky intervals which this one fault gave rise to.   In due
course of time the father of the lady departed this
life, and among other heirlooms that reverted to her,
was a clock which had literally served its time in the
family.   In the days of her early childhood, she who
was now an unpunctual wife, had been led to regard
this clock as a monitor who was to be implicitly
obeyed.   Her going to and returning from school,
her bed-time, her play-time, her meal-time, were
duly regarded as they were duly recorded.   And she
would no more have thought of questioning the
fidelity of this Time's chronicler, than she would the
word of her parents themselves.   Now, when this
clock once more made its appearance among the household gods, the old feeling of veneration and regard returned, and asserted its supremacy as strongly in the
bosom of the matron as it had reigned in the breast
of the child.   Forthwith every household duty was
performed and regulated by this faithful indicator.
The husband was not long in noting this new-born
love of punctuality, nor slow in tracing the cause of
it.   He determined on profiting by it to the furthest
extent, to compensate himself for many terrible disappointments hitherto experienced, and to make provision for any future relapse.   He accordingly hit
upon the expedient of privately putting on the clock
a quarter of an hour, and keeping it thus in advance
without his wife's knowledge in perpetuity.   This he
successfully accomplished; and although occasional

droppers-in sometimes ventured to hint that the clock was a little fast, and although every other time-piece far and near appeared by comparison to be slow, the good lady remained true to her horological faith, and to the latest day of her existence held the belief that of all the clocks in the universe, hers only was right, and every other wrong. It is needless to remark on the advantage which was not only reaped by the husband, but which accrued to the parties concerned by this harmless ruse.

To resume the thread of our remarks, there certainly cannot be exhibited a more ludicrous sight than that presented by a man vainly endeavouring to catch the train. If he be burdened by many packages, and accompanied by a wife and a numerous family of young children, the picture is considerably heightened. Under any circumstance, it is galling enough to make that frantic rush amidst the clattering of wheels, the barking of dogs, the jeers of bystanders, and the grim smiles of railway officials, and all this with no other result than to see the train you have made such desperate exertions to save, quietly steaming out of the station, to say nothing of the irksomeness of being imprisoned, perhaps, at some out-of-the-way station, for two or three hours, and the humiliation of being regarded and alluded to as "the party that was too late for the last train." Even supposing that by a happy chance the train is just saved, the traveller is huddled into the first vacant seat without being allowed to exercise choice. He is very hot, flurried, and certainly not in the most amiable of moods. The probabilities are that he has

lost or left something behind, or if he has not, he is
under that impression, and is in a state of considerable agitation accordingly.   Therefore we say,
if you wish to start on a journey comfortably, or,
indeed, if you desire to start at all—*Be in time.*

TRAVELLING COSTUME.

The dress which a person wears when travelling
by railway, need not be an object of solicitude so far
as fashion is concerned; the end to be achieved is
comfort and ease. For gentlemen, the best costume
is one of those suits now so commonly worn, made of
the same material, fashioned in such a manner as to
leave the body and limbs free and unconstrained, and
the colour light, so as not to show the dust, nor require constant brushing; moreover, liberally furnished
with pockets for books, newspapers, sandwiches,
pocket-flask, etc. One of the most sensible articles
of travelling attire is a shirt of flannel, which is much
warmer than the linen or cotton shirt ordinarily worn,
and does away with the necessity of frequent change of
garment, which entails upon the traveller considerable
expense and inconvenience. It will also be found a
good plan in many cases to wear patent leather boots
instead of the ordinary leather ones : they can be
cleaned by the wearer himself with a little oil or
milk, and are always at hand. A cap is preferable to
a hat ; but if the traveller be wedded to the chimney-
pot style of head-covering, he had better provide himself with a " gibus," or compressible hat, which admits
of being easily stowed away when not in use. It would

be as well for the traveller to provide himself with an over-coat, no matter what the season, the weight of the garment being regulated accordingly. In our variable climate sunshine may at any moment be interrupted by rain; and even in the height of summer keen blasts and cold winds sometimes make themselves felt. To meet these contingencies, the secret, therefore, is to have an over-coat which is not heavy to carry either on the back or in the hand, serving its purpose when required, and not proving burdensome when no longer needed. Over-coats possessing these qualifications are made in great variety. It is of the utmost importance to keep the feet warm; this may be accomplished by a pair of lamb's-wool socks and thick-soled boots, a pair of extra socks drawn over the ordinary ones, cork soles cr strips of flannel placed within the boots. For effectually protecting the body against cold there is nothing better than a maud or shepherd's plaid. For keeping away draughts from the legs a railway rug or wrapper will answer the desired end. We shall perhaps be excused for calling attention to a new material for wearing apparel which will possibly prove of service to the railway traveller; we allude to paper. There are now being advertised paper collars, paper shirt-fronts, paper waistcoats, etc. The novelty is perhaps too startling to meet with general and immediate adoption; and besides the material is generally regarded as too fragile to be depended on. A gentleman presenting himself at the dinner-table with a white paper waistcoat washed into a pulp, would cut a rather ignominious figure; a shirt-front torn in the centre

would somewhat awkwardly reveal the secrets of the
bosom, and there would be something extremely un-
dignified in dog-eared wristbands. In the matter of
collars, however, there is not so much to object to.
They will doubtless serve their purpose for the day,
and inasmuch as their cost is not greater than the
charge for washing linen ones, they will be found
more convenient and equally as economical. The traveller thus provided with these, and with the flannel
shirts previously referred to, may travel from place to
place without being irritated by that somewhat un-
certain and exacting class — the laundresses. As
regards ladies' attire, we dare scarcely enter within
that penetralia. We may, however, be excused for
recommending the use of a veil for protecting the face
and eyes; and a general regard for comfort and convenience rather than appearances.

SUPPLY OF ETCETERAS.

It has been said that with a shilling, a piece of
string, and a pocket-knife a man is prepared for any
emergency. Without bounding our view within this
narrow limit, we are of opinion that the possession of
a few articles, comparatively trifling in themselves, is
calculated to enhance the comfort and convenience of
the railway traveller. Supposing the railway traveller
to be provided—as we trust every railway traveller is
—with a liberal supply of cash, there is even here a
consideration as to its most available form. If the
sum required be not very large, we strongly advise
that it should be in hard cash, for this is readily trans-

mittable. If notes must be necessarily taken, they should be of the smallest amount, as great difficulty and even expense is sometimes incurred in procuring change for larger notes. And even where the change can be given, it is in many cases withheld, because there exists a lurking suspicion that all is not right. Neither should a supply of small change be wanting, half-crowns, shillings, sixpences, fourpenny pieces, etc., ready for all calls and claims. When a traveller is unprovided with this comparatively trifling material, it is astonishing how liable he renders himself to overcharges and impositions; and frequently, rather than be put to annoyance and delay, he has to pay four or five times the value of an article or for trifling services performed. Before starting on a journey, therefore, we would advise that change be sent for, and a portion of it, comprising every variety of coin, placed loose in the pocket for instant disbursement. Every person of ordinary thought and observation should carry with him a pocket memorandum book; many incidents may occur well worthy of note, many items of information may present themselves which should in no case pass by unrecorded. And here we would impress upon the reader not to be afraid or ashamed of using such a book, and not to trust too implicitly to memory to retain all that is seen and heard. If in an ordinary railway journey, say from London to York, a passenger were to jot down actual observations, and passing impressions, he could not fail to be surprised and pleased hereafter with the fund of profit and pleasure he had thus stored up. No person should travel by railway without

having his card of address about him, setting aside
the painful catastrophe of an accident, there are numerous emergencies when this simple voucher of
respectability and personal identity is calculated to
play an important part, and in the absence of which,
it is just possible for a person to be regarded with
suspicion, treated with indignity, and, for a time,
even deprived of his liberty. The most immaculate
of railway travellers may bear an unfortunate resem-
blance to an accomplished swindler who once came by
the same route, or be the very counterpart of some
notorious offender, "wanted," in the *Hue and Cry*.
True, the possession of a card of address would not be
in itself sufficient evidence of innocence and respectability, but this would go far to establish the truth,
and, taken in connection with corroborative testimony,
would probably clear up all doubts. Occasion frequently arises for despatching a written communication at some point of the journey, or before the
traveller is fairly established in his quarters. Under
such circumstances, it is very difficult, and sometimes impossible, to procure writing materials, postage
stamps, etc. As a provision against such emergencies, it is to be recommended that the traveller carry in his pocket-book three or four sheets
of note-paper folded within as many envelopes, and
with postage stamps affixed; these, with a pocket-pen
and a small inkstand so constructed as not to allow
the ink to escape, will place it in the possessor's power
to write a note at any moment, and to despatch it
through the next post-office arrived at. When it is
borne in mind how frequently such emergencies as

these arise, how important it is that they should be immediately attended to, how small the bulk of the articles mentioned, how easily procured, and how handy at all times and all places, we need offer no further apology for laying some stress on this matter.

CONVEYANCE TO THE STATION.

The railway traveller will seldom experience any difficulty in meeting with a conveyance to take him to the station. Omnibusses, cabs, flys, etc., customarily journey stationwards conformably with the departure and arrival of the various trains, while in the streets of London, and other large cities, a vehicle is always within hail. If a person has little or no luggage, a seat in an omnibus will answer his purpose, but if his packages are numerous, then it will be necessary to have a cab or a fly. The squabbles between drivers and their fares upon alighting are matters of notoriety, and generally follow as a matter of course. But this is especially the case when a person is conveyed to a railway station, for the cabman well knows that ninety-nine persons out of a hundred prefer paying the excess of fare to missing the train, which they are likely to do by contending against the overcharge. The most satisfactory plan is to bargain with the driver before setting out, telling him exactly how many persons and packages there are, so that he may have no pretext for claiming extra fare. But if this be not done, it should be known that at most stations there is exhibited a table of fares, calculated from several points, and if this fail in affording the desired

information, the policeman, or head porter on duty,
will generally be able to throw a light on the matter.
In any case, be prepared with the exact amount of
the fare, for cabmen resemble, in this particular, Gold-
smith's Village Preacher, who

> " Ne'er had changed, nor wished to change."

If you have but a short time to reach the station
in, be careful to choose a cab with a fresh-looking
horse attached to it, and not one where the animal,
either from deficiency of nutriment, or excess of
labour, is in such a drooping condition as to render
him obviously unequal to the contemplated task. The
Hansom cabs are generally the most expeditious, but
Clarence cabs are best adapted for quantities of luggage. If you determine upon walking to the station,
allow yourself a few moments' grace beyond the bare
time required. Observe, also, not to take any short
cuts, unless you well know the road, for such attempts
at abridging the distance frequently end in extending
it, and sometimes result in losing the train. If you
miss your way, or are in doubt, press the first intelligent lad you meet with into your service, and for a
few pence he will cheerfully conduct you to the wished-
for goal. In cases where persons reside some miles
from the station, and where the passengers and luggage
are sufficient to fill two or three cabs or flys, it is a
very good plan to charter an omnibus expressly for
the journey; this will not prove any more expensive,
and infinitely more convenient. If your effects are
very numerous and bulky, sufficient, for instance, to
fill a van, the railway company, on being written to,

will despatch one of their vans to your address, and in this, the goods will be packed by the company's servants, and conveyed just as it is on to the rails of the line, where it will be either attached to the train you travel by, or to some other train, according to special arrangement. This will prevent much loading and unloading, expense, damage, loss, and confusion. In the course of his peregrinations, the railway traveller may find himself in some out-of-the-way place, where no regular vehicle can be obtained to convey him to the station, and this *contretemp* is aggravated when the time of departure happens to be early in the morning; in such a dilemma, a mail-cart, a market-cart, or some such conveyance, may come to the traveller's rescue. And this knowledge may be ga-thered at the village ale-house, the grocer's, the post-office, etc. Captain B——, a man of restless energy and adventurous spirit, emerged early one morning from a hovel in a distant village, where from stress of weather he had been compelled to pass the night. It was just dawn of day, and within an hour the train he wished to go by would start from the station, about six miles distant. He had with him a portmanteau, which it would be impossible for him to carry within the prescribed time, but which he could not very well leave behind. Pondering on what he should do, his eye lighted on a likely-looking horse grazing in a field hard by, while in the next field there was a line ex-tended between two posts, for the purpose of drying clothes on. The sight of these objects soon suggested the plan for him to adopt. In an instant he detached the line, and then taking a piece of bread from his

pocket, coaxed the animal to approach him. Captain
B—— was an adept in the management of horses, and
as a rough-rider, perhaps, had no equal. In a few
seconds he had, by the aid of a portion of the line,
arranged his portmanteau pannier-wise across the
horse's back, and forming a bridle with the remaining
portion of the line; he led his steed into the lane, and
sprang upon his back. The horse rather relished the
trip than otherwise, and what with the unaccustomed
burden, and the consciousness that he was being
steered by a knowing hand, he sped onwards at a
terrific pace. While in mid career, one of the mounted
police espied the captain coming along the road at a
distance; recognizing the horse, but not knowing the
rider, and noticing also the portmanteau, and the
uncouth equipment, this rural guardian of the peace
at once came to the conclusion that this was a case
of robbery and horse-stealing; as the captain neared
him, he endeavoured to stop him, and stretched forth
his hand to seize the improvized bridle, but the gallant
equestrian laughed to scorn this impotent attempt,
and shook him off, and shot by him. Thus foiled, the
policeman had nothing to do than to give chase; so
turning his horse's head he followed in full cry. The
clatter and shouts of pursuer and pursued brought
forth the inhabitants of the cottages they passed, and
many of these joined in the chase. Never since
Turpin's ride to York, or Johnny Gilpin's ride to
Edmonton, had there been such a commotion caused
by an equestrian performance. To make a long story
short, the captain reached the station in ample time;
an explanation ensued; a handsome apology was

tendered to the patrol, and a present equally handsome was forwarded, together with the abstracted property, to the joint owner of the horse and the clothes-line.

ARRIVAL AT THE STATION.

Supposing you to arrive at the station in a cab, you will there find a porter ready to remove the luggage on to his truck; superintend this removal, see that you have all your packages, give a glance inside the cab to ascertain that nothing is left behind, and as a further precaution note the number of the driver in case anything should have escaped your notice. If you are accompanied by any persons, conduct them to the waiting-room, there to remain until you come for them after having settled the preliminaries of the journey. Although the railway company have now charge of your luggage, you are still expected to exercise supervision over it to prevent its being mislaid or missent. Therefore, after having conducted your travelling companions to the waiting-room, you return to look after the luggage which is in the hall, or may have been in the meantime wheeled on to the station. When you recognize the truck upon which your effects are deposited, you call the attention of one of the porters to it, and he will wheel the things to the proper department, where a printed label of the name of the place you are destined for will be affixed upon each package. This process is an important one, and ought to be personally superintended by every owner of luggage. While this is being done, you may select

the smaller articles or those you may wish to have
with you in the carriage. The next duty is to see
your luggage stowed away, making a memorandum of
the number of the van in which or upon which the
luggage is placed; while to facilitate your lighting
upon the van at the end of the journey without
hesitation, it would be as well to remark its relative
position from the engine; and thus note it in your memorandum book, " Luggage in van No. ——, the —th
carriage from the engine." We have now to notice
the quantity of luggage which each person is entitled
to carry with him free of charge. In this particular
there is a slight variation between the different Lines;
those which run their trains to commercial and manufacturing districts are more liberal in their allowance
than those lines which convey chiefly pleasure seekers;
for instance, the Great Northern allows first class,
112 lbs.; second class, 100 lbs.; third class, 56 lbs.;
while the South Eastern stipulates for first class,
100 lbs.; second class, 60 lbs.; third class, 56 lbs.
The average quantity of luggage allowed on the various
railroads may be calculated to be between these two
extreme rates. It will here be seen what an advantage the light leather travelling equipage of modern
days possess over the heavy and lumbering trunks
of a former age. The truth is, that owing to the
difficulties and expenses of travelling, our forefathers
were more settled in their habits than we are; they
contented themselves with a journey perhaps once in
seven years; we, on the contrary, deem it not excessive to take seven journeys in one year. If a lynx-
eyed railway porter suspects that a railway traveller

has a larger amount of luggage than he ought to have, he settles his suspicions by an appeal to the weighing machine, and for every pound of luggage in excess a charge is made at a certain rate. This excess the owner has the option of taking with him by the same train, or of sending by a "goods train," which is cheaper than an ordinary passenger train. If, however, his luggage is comprised in one large package, he must perforce take it with him, and submit to pay the higher rate. It is an excellent plan, where a person has a much greater extent of luggage than he knows he can take with him, to send the quantity in excess a day or two previously by a goods train, directing it to be left at the station till called for, or sending it to some friend or acquaintance to take charge of for a few days. On some lines, passengers by express trains are not permitted to carry the same weight of luggage as passengers by ordinary trains, on other lines no such distinction is made; but this point should be clearly ascertained by the traveller beforehand. Travellers by ordinary excursion trains are not allowed to take with them luggage, properly so called, what they may take being restricted to such sized packages as can be conveniently stowed away in the carriage by which they travel.

CHOICE OF ROUTE.

Many places may be reached by three or four routes, the competition among the various companies prompting them to annex such and such towns to their line at whatever cost or sacrifice. These bids for the patronage of railway travellers exercise an appreciable influence on the comfort and convenience offered, and the rate of fares charged. The various routes also afford passengers an agreeable change, and give them the opportunity of judging which is the most desirable line to travel by. When, therefore, a person is about to proceed to a certain place, he should ascertain whether it is accessible by more routes than one, and if it be so, he should compare the several fares charged, the relative distances, the time occupied in the journey, the number of stations stopped at, etc. Some regard is also to be had to the direct or indirect nature of the route. For although the fare in one case may be lower than the other, yet there may be involved change of carriage, halting at junctions, and other disagreeable hitches, which are more exacting than the mere disbursement of a few extra shillings. Excursionists who are not bound to any particular place, but to whom all points of the compass are alike, will do well to study attentively the excursion schemes put forth by the various companies, for by exercising this selection a more pleasurable excursion at a much less cost may be devised than could be obtained by hasty adoption. Another consideration in the choice of lines is the proximity of the terminus to the town. In the one case the station may be situated in the very centre of the place; in the other it may be some miles distant. The time lost, and the extra expense in the latter case forming important considerations.

CHOICE OF TRAIN.

On every railroad there are trains running at certain rates, and distinguished by some speciality. First in importance is the special train; and although this does not apply to the public generally, still it is as well to know that on great emergencies, and in matters of life and death, a train may be despatched to any point, and placed entirely at the disposal of the person or persons demanding the convenience; they, of course, defraying the extraordinary charge, which is necessarily a heavy one. When a special train is required, the usual method is to apply to the station-master, who will at once put the matter in hand. The express train takes second rank as a class of conveyance. The speed at which this train goes is very great; thirty, forty, and sometimes fifty miles an hour being attained. Very few stations are called at, the object being to perform the journey as quickly and with as few interruptions as possible. The express has seldom a third class attached to it, and in some cases consists of first class only. There is usually some limit with regard to luggage, and the fare is higher than by ordinary train, ranging from an eighth to a fourth more. This train is well adapted for business persons, or for those bent on any pressing errand. The times of departure are usually between nine and ten in the morning, and between four and five in the afternoon. At the first blush it would appear that a train travelling at the tremendous pace indicated is peculiarly liable to meet with accident, whereas the exact reverse is the case. The engine selected for the express train, the carriages the most secure, and the *employés* the most intelligent and trustworthy which the management can select. Then every precaution is taken to avoid collision with other trains, and the advent of the express is signalled from station to station along the whole route. Finally, the extraordinary momentum which is attained, enables the train to dash through interposing obstacles without communicating scarcely any shock to the passengers, whereas an ordinary train under the same circumstances would experience a concussion, resulting in all probability in the loss of life and limb. But to many persons the excessive vibration felt when travelling by express is most disagreeable, and when it is remembered how violently the body is thrown from side to side, and every now and then pitched in an opposite direction, and this incessantly for perhaps three or four hours, it is not to be wondered at that the delicate and ailing who have been subjected to such a process should feel *shaky* for some days afterwards. The mail train is preferred by many persons travelling on business, for inasmuch as it is employed in the postal service, its movements are necessarily regulated by the most scrupulous punctuality. The mere idea of travelling by the same train as the mail imparts a kind of confidence in the superior efficiency of the locomotive arrangements. The drawback with regard to the train is that it travels by night, generally departing at nine o'clock in the evening, and arriving at its destination in the " small hours." The parliamentary train, so called because, according to act of Parliament, every line is compelled to despatch a train at least once daily, by which passengers shall travel at the rate of one penny per mile. It need scarcely be stated that as this is the cheapest, so is it the slowest mode of railway conveyance. Its maximum rate of speed is seldom greater than twenty miles an hour, and in some instances considerably less. It stops at all the stations. The time of departure is usually early in the morning, so that a person having a distance of more than a hundred miles to go may calculate upon passing the best part of the day on the rail. Although the parliamentary train is obviously tedious to many persons, yet there are others for whom it has its advantages. The slow pace and the frequent stoppages adapt themselves to the exigencies of invalids, and tend to quiet the apprehensions of the timid. Excursion trains, although a great boon to the humbler classes and the economically inclined, are not best calculated for the ordinary traveller. The confusion and bustle, the irregular times of departure and arrival, and the boisterous company into which one is thrown, although of very little moment to the person who has only a travelling bag, and who sets out for a few days' jaunt, are ill-calculated for the railway traveller who has a sober journey to perform, and is burdened with its attendant responsibilities and cares.

RAILWAY PRIVILEGES.

Every inducement to travel, in the form of fares and accommodation, is held out by the various railway companies. First of all we have the return-ticket, enabling the traveller to accomplish the double journey at the rate of about a fare and a-half. These tickets are in some cases limited to use on the day on which they are issued; while in other instances an interval of two or three days is allowed. The season-ticket or annual-ticket, payable monthly or quarterly, acts as a great encouragement for persons to become permanent residents in country places accessible by rail. The rate at which this privilege can be secured, is probably one-half or one-third less than would be paid in the ordinary way. It permits the person to travel as often as he pleases by any train, and to or from any part of the line. It also obviates the inconvenience and delay occasionally experienced in procuring the ticket, the holder of the season-ticket having nothing more to do than to make straight for the carriage.

We may here remind season-ticket holders to renew their privilege when the current term has expired; the omitting to do this, either by accident or design, and still travelling on the line, has before now led to awkward exposures and unpleasant consequences. Through-tickets are issued to enable travellers to take a certain route from one point to another, and to stop at various intermediate places. Before such ticket is taken, the intending railway traveller should make sure that he will be entitled to stop at those places he desires to visit, and he should also explicitly understand what interval of time is allowed him at each halting-place.

Excursion-tickets are of varied kind and character; the leading idea is, however, to afford an opportunity of enjoying the greatest amount of pleasure at the smallest possible cost. Sometimes there are certain restrictions which excursionists are expected to pay attention to and abide by. As, for instance, a limit in the quantity of luggage; not being allowed to stop at intermediate stations; being obliged to travel by certain trains, and none others, etc.

RAILWAY INSURANCE.

There is a certain amount of hazard in railway travelling, and although the number of accidents are few, when taken in connection with the immense amount of traffic, nevertheless, there are such unfortunate occurrences, and they may visit any person at any period. One person may take long journeys, day after day, and year after year, and escape for a time on the principle that "the pitcher that goes often to the well is broken at last." Another person may perhaps venture on a railway for the first time in his life, and meet with an untimely end. One of the characteristics of railway accidents is that the injuries sustained are for the most part severe, and when not fatal, frequently incapacitating the sufferer from pursuing any active business during the remainder of his life-time. Sometimes the accident is of so peculiar a nature, that although there is no external appearance of injury, yet the shock given to the system has been so violent as to interrupt the functions of the brain, disturb the equilibrium of the mind, and even to suspend vitality itself. To meet such catastrophes as these, there exists a Railway Passengers' Assurance Company, which undertakes to pay compensation in cases of accident or death, upon the following principles :—Insurances may be effected for a single or a double journey, for periods of time from one to twelve months ; for terms of five or ten years; for the whole term of life. The system of insuring for each journey is conducted at nearly all railway stations, by the traveller taking an insurance ticket of the booking clerk at the time of taking the railway journey-ticket. The addition to the railway fare is very trifling, namely, one penny for the third class, twopence for the second class, and threepence for the first-class, whatever may be the length of the journey. The sums insured for these payments are £1000 to a first-class passenger ; £500 to a second-class passenger ; and £200 to a third-class passenger. These amounts are paid in case of death, and proportionate compensation allowed in cases of personal injury. The same amounts can be insured for a double or return journey, and for excursion trains, at corresponding rates of premiums. Insurances for periods of time may be also effected at the various railway stations, securing compensation for death or accident occurring on any railway in the United Kingdom, or on the Continent of Europe, namely, to insure £1000, a premium of £5 for one month ; £10 for three months ; £16 for six months ; £20 for twelve months. Annual insurance may be effected by the payment of a small premium yearly ; and insurance for a term of years by a single payment at a proportionally low rate.

The easy and ready manner in which these insurances may be effected, leaves no excuse for the railway traveller neglecting to take so wise a precaution. All that has to be done is to place the insurance fee along with the railway fare on the pay-counter, and to receive the insurance-ticket with the railway-ticket. Against this mode of insurance as against others, some weak-minded persons are prejudiced, because they fear that the very catastrophe against which they are providing will be all the more likely to occur; an illogical and unfounded mode of reasoning unworthy alike of argument or refutation. One important feature of railway-insurance is, that compensation paid by the insurance company does not invalidate any claim that may be made on the railway company; and in the event of an action being brought, the payment of such compensation cannot be pleaded in mitigation of damages. Supposing the railway traveller to have insured for the journey he is about to take, the next consideration is the disposal of the insurance-ticket. It is not safe for him to retain it about his person, because in the event of an accident the ticket may be destroyed, or may fall out of the pocket and be lost; thus precluding either the sufferer or his survivors reaping the contemplated benefit. The best plan is, therefore, for the railway traveller to take with him an envelope stamped and addressed to his wife, or nearest and dearest friend, to insert the ticket in this envelope, and to post it either at the station, or at an office in the immediate locality. Or if he be accompanied by a friend, he may hand the ticket over to him without any further trouble. But if these little matters are objected to as distracting the attention and harassing the mind of the traveller at the important moment of starting, then let him insure by the year or for a term, thus becoming a policy-holder, as in the case of ordinary life insurance.

CHOICE OF CLASS.

The three classes of railway travelling may be said to correspond with the degrees of comparison, positive, comparative, superlative. He who regards economy as of paramount importance, he who aims at combining respectability with moderate charge, or he who is indifferent to cost, and studies his comfort only, is duly catered and cared for. At the time when lotteries were in vogue, a person of low estate purchased a ticket; on the day when a list of the prizes was posted up at the lottery-office, he proceeded thither to ascertain his fate, and to his great joy and astonishment beheld the number of his ticket adjudged a £20,000 prize. To calm the agitation of his mind, produced by this event, he determined upon taking a walk round St. Paul's, and during that short promenade, he settled within himself the manner in which he should expend his newly-acquired fortune. His walk ended, he thought he would just go to the lottery-office again, to feast his eyes on the agreeable announcement. But, oh, horror! on reading over the list, he found that his ticket was no longer included among the fortunate numbers. In a state of bewilderment bordering on distraction, he entered the lottery-office to inquire into the discrepancy; the matter was soon explained: by a slip of the pen one little figure had been substituted for another, thus entirely altering the context, and raising false hopes. The victim of this blunder was often heard to declare, that the ten minutes of ecstasy which he enjoyed under the impression that he was a man of fortune, more than compensated for years of actual poverty, and to the day of his death he persisted in declaring he had once been worth £20,000. The relevancy of this anecdote is, that the meanest of mankind may, as a railway traveller, taste for once in his life the luxury and ease supposed to be the peculiar privilege of the rich and great, and, providing he occupy the compartment alone, he may boast in after life that he once rode in his own carriage.

Let us now glance at the comparative cost and comfort of the three classes. The fare of the first class is usually one-third more than that of the second class, and double that of the third class. But the superior accommodation is more than commensurate with the excess of fare. The carriage is unexceptionably fitted up, and the occupants polite and well conducted. It is said that a greater amount of respect is accorded to the occupants of first class carriages than to others; and *Punch* once presented to his readers a kind of gamut or scale of railway civility, as thus: *Collector of tickets* (*to first class passengers*), "May I trouble you for your tickets?" (*To second class*), "Tickets, please." (*To third class*), "Now then! tickets." We, however, who have always found railway servants uniformly civil and obliging, have no complaint to urge on this score. First class travelling is undoubtedly most suitable for ladies, and for delicate or sickly

persons. In the latter case, especially, it should be
borne in mind that the excess of fare is trifling as
compared with the probable doctor's charges, conse-
quent upon a cold caught by an invalid journeying in
second or third class. Another recommendation of
the first class is, that the carriages are never over-
crowded, and even if they have their complement of
passengers, there is still ample sitting room, without
any of that crowding, jostling, or edging, which are so
peculiarly irritating. For the enjoyment of ease and
comfort in the highest degree, we would commend
the traveller to what are termed the saloon carriages,
for in these a person may recline with perfect freedom
and may shift his position as often as he pleases,
without incommoding or annoying his fellow-traveller.
The second class fare is usually one-fourth less than
the first class, but the difference in comfort is immense. The seats and backs of the ordinary second
class carriage are of wood, and the travelling with
these surroundings, for any length of time, is of the
most unpleasant description. There is, in point of
fact, but little distinction between second and third
class, the main difference being in the quality of the
company. It is to be observed, however, that on
some lines the second class carriages do not answer to
the general description; an attempt is made to render
them comfortable, and the seats are partially cushioned.
But even this occasional concession would appear to
be a matter of caprice, for some trains run the better
sort of carriages, while other trains, even on the same
line, adhere to the inferior kind. The far-seeing and
provident traveller, therefore, will do well if, pre-

viously to taking his ticket, he run his eye along the
departing train, and ascertain whether the possibility
exists of his having something approximating to first
class comfort at second class fare. The discomforts
and inconveniences of the third class are too notorious
to need much dwelling upon. Of course, the lowness
of fare is the grand recommendation, but even in this
particular, a return journey can be performed at a
cheaper rate by second class than by third, inasmuch
as return-tickets are not generally issued for the
latter. Some persons, attracted by the lowness of
fare, and unacquainted with the attendant drawbacks,
have an inclination to ride by third class. Under
such circumstances they may be destined to pass the
next few hours of their existence tightly compressed
between two rough specimens of humanity. They
may be doomed to semi-suffocation, to partial extinc-
tion of vision, and total deprivation of motive power
by several large bundles, boxes, or baskets, which every
other passenger insists upon carrying, and which no
amount of force or persuasion can apparently induce
them to relinquish. It may be that the shoulders,
shins, toes, or other parts of the body, will from time
to time be brought into contact with angularities or
cubes. Let us be understood as not deriding third
class passengers, but as merely pointing out that these
little rubs, which are patiently borne by the humbler
and more enduring portion of the community, may
prove a source of great disquiet and pain to him who
is unaccustomed to be thus tried.

To sum up the respective merits of the various modes
of railway travelling, we should say, let all persons who

can afford it travel first class, and let even those who imagine they cannot do so, and who have a long distance to go, expend a few extra shillings in this direction, and economize them in some other. For short journeys, however, the second class may be ridden by without any material sacrifice of comfort, and for very short journeys, where a person wishes to view the country, enjoy the breeze, and indulge in a cigar, the third class will answer the purpose sufficiently well. The assertion may appear a startling one, that a person cannot always travel by the class he would wish, but is compelled, by that regard for appearances which influences society at large, to ride by the dearer class, when his means are better suited to an inferior class. This is an important consideration for persons who are about to take season-tickets, and who will, in all probability, have occasion to travel frequently in company with those with whom they are associated by commercial or social ties, and when to travel by an inferior class would argue either poverty or meanness. Here is a case in point: a London merchant resided a few miles from the City, in an elegant mansion, to and from which he journeyed daily, and invariably by third class. It happened that one of the clerks in his employ lived in a cottage accessible by the same line of railway, but he always travelled first class; the same train thus presenting the anomaly of the master being in that place which one would naturally assign to the man, and the man appearing to usurp the position of the master. One day these two alighted at the terminus in full view of each other. "Well," said Mr. B——, in that tone of banter which a superior so frequently thinks it becoming to adopt. " I don't know how you manage to ride first class, when in these hard times I find third class fare as much as I can afford." " Sir," replied the clerk, " you, who are known to be a person of wealth and position, may adopt the most economical mode of travelling at no worse risk than being thought eccentric, and even with the applause of some for your manifest absence of pride. But, as for myself, I cannot afford to indulge in such irregularities. Among the persons I travel with I am reported to be a well-paid *employé*, and am respected accordingly; to maintain this reputation I am compelled to travel in the same manner as they do, and were I to adopt an inferior mode, it would be attributed to some serious falling off of income; a circumstance which would occasion me not only loss of consideration among my *quondam* fellow-travellers, but one which, upon coming to the ears of my butcher, baker, and grocer, might seriously injure my credit with those highly respectable, but certainly worldly-minded, tradesmen." Mr. B—— was not slow in recognizing the full force of this argument, more particularly as the question of his own liberality was involved, nor did he hesitate to give it a practical application by immediately increasing the salary of his clerk, not only to the amount of a first class season-ticket, but something over.

CHOICE OF CARRIAGE.

In the selection of his carriage, the railway traveller has to take into consideration both comfort and security. The old stager is fully alive to this, and makes his choice with as much deliberation as an alderman would select his port. His decision being influenced by actual experience, as follows:—The middle of the train is the safest, because in the event of being run into from behind, or meeting a train in front, the force of the concussion would, in either case, be considerably expended before the centre part were reached. The carriages nearest the engine are regarded as dangerous in case of an accident occurring to the engine itself, or in the event of its running off the line, when it usually manages to drag the next two or three carriages with it. The tail of the train is not liked, because it moves—in summer-time especially—in a perpetual cloud of dust, which is not calculated to improve the attire or benefit the lungs. The oscillation, jerking, and other eccentric movements of the train are also felt with greater force at the end than in any other portion; and it does sometimes happen that the last carriage or two, by the severance of the coupling-irons, become separated from their travelling companions, and are left standing stock-still on the line, while the forward portion of the train speeds on its way unconscious of, and therefore unheeding, the catastrophe.

Observe that the first-class carriages lined with cloth are warmer than those lined with leather or horsehair; therefore, in winter the former are the most comfortable; in summer the latter are coolest. If you wish to recline at full length, and have reason to believe that the carriage will not fill, one having no division of seats may be selected, but under ordinary

BEFORE THE JOURNEY. 59

circumstances the carriages having divisions are the most comfortable, as they afford a great support to the body when in a sitting position, and effectually prevent persons monopolizing an undue share of space. If there are two kinds of second-class carriages, the one having ample window-room, and the other with a small opening on each side resembling port-holes, avoid the latter as you would the plague, especially if the weather be hot, unless you wish to realize to yourself what the terrible position might have been of those unfortunate occupants of the Black Hole of Calcutta. When you are going on a long journey, bring the principles of Lavater to your aid, and scan the features of the persons already in possession of the carriage, with a view of ascertaining whether they are likely to prove pleasant travelling companions or the contrary. Life is so short, that even a few hours miserably or happily spent are objects of consequence. Do not select a carriage which is obviously already in the possession of a party, the forming "one too many" is anything but agreeable. A conversation carried on across you and behind you, and upon topics in which you are in no way concerned, is apt to prove uninteresting. Then there is that system of private telegraphing from one to the other, which might be interpreted thus, "What a nuisance, this man coming in our carriage!" "If he had any sense he might have known that he wasn't wanted here." "Did ever you see such a guy—I wonder who and what he is," and so on. So if a party wish to travel in perfect comfort, and to keep together, they should engage a carriage for their exclusive occupation, and this might be done by sending word to the station-master a day or two previously, and to insure attention, forwarding at the same time the amount of fare.

CHOICE OF SEAT.

The most comfortable seat in a railway carriage is a corner one, and if you desire to be undisturbed and at the same time to have an opportunity of viewing the country, the corner furthest from the door at which the passengers enter, is the best. If, however, you have not far to go, or wish to witness the bustle and commotion of the platform, then take up your station at the corner nearest the entrance door. It is generally acknowledged that sitting with the back to the engine prevents the motion of the carriage being felt in a great degree, but to some persons this makes no difference. Certainly, in sitting with the back towards the engine, one escapes the dust and ashes which are constantly flying about. The centre compartment of a first-class carriage is said to be safest in the event of a collision, because this portion of the carriage is more substantially built, and consequently better calculated to resist the shock.

In second and third-class carriages avoid sitting near the doorway; the constant opening and shutting of the door subject those near it to cold and draughts, and the incessant passing to and fro, with the usual accompaniments of shoulder-grasping and toe-crushing, is more than sufficient to test the best of tempers. It also frequently happens that one of the passengers, a "navvy," for instance, is ever and anon thrusting his head out the window, thus favouring you with an uninterrupted view of his substantial but by no means picturesque proportions, and at the same time beating time on your shins with his hob-nailed and iron-shod high-lows.

SENDING FEMALES AND CHILDREN BY RAILWAY UNACCOMPANIED.

It frequently happens that a female is compelled to undertake a journey by railway unaccompanied. She can generally contrive, however, to secure the services of her husband, brother, or other male relative to see her off by the train; and as the departure is the most harassing part of the journey, she will then not have much to dread. In such a case we would advise the person who has charge of the lady, to put her into a carriage where there are others of her own sex, especially those of matronly appearance, and with family surroundings; they might be asked in a respectful manner if they were going as far as the unaccompanied female. Any woman of ordinary shrewdness and kindly feeling would understand the question, and determine within her own mind to extend the required protection. But a person of tact could manage this matter in a better way. He might enter into conversation with the ladies, and incidentally mention that her companion was compelled to travel alone; then after a few other remarks he might claim their protection, and having thus established a sort of introduction, leave the future fellow-travellers to improve the occasion. If a female is obliged not only to travel alone, but to go to the station alone, she should place herself under the care of one of the policemen or guards, of whom she will find many, and he will see her luggage stowed away, assist her in procuring a ticket, in selecting a seat, etc.

In some extreme cases it is necessary to send a child of tender years by railway without a protector. There was an account in the newspapers some time since of a little boy, seven years of age, being despatched alone from York to London, a label, inscribed with his name and address and destination, was attached to his clothes, with no further direction than that he was to wait at the terminus till called for. The account goes on to state that this strange living package was conveyed "with care," and that he arrived at the place to which he was sent in perfect safety. We do not altogether advocate such a mode of despatch as this, but we would advise a person having to send a child unaccompanied by railway, to place him in a carriage where there is a family party, so that he will stand a chance not only of being protected but amused in company with those of his own age. Under any circumstances, the bare mention of such a fact to even the most inexorable of bachelors, would prove a sufficient claim on his sympathies, and induce him to treat his little travelling companion with kindness and consideration. The attention of the guard might be also drawn to the circumstance, who would see every now and then how Master Halfprice was getting on, and thus the journey would be accomplished in safety.

RETAINING SEAT.

So soon as the railway traveller is admitted to the platform, he should hasten to the train drawn alongside, and having first ascertained that it is the train he is to proceed by, at once select his carriage and seat according to the hints previously given. If he have companions, then the choice must be made with a view to the comfort of all; if he has only himself to please, the task is extremely simple. There is a certain etiquette in connection with the retaining of seats which it is considered both rude and unjust to disregard. Thus, the placing of a coat, a book, a newspaper, or any other article, on the seat of a carriage, is intended as a token that such place is engaged. This principle is to be acted on in the retaining of seats, and, whatever the number you require, should have deposited conspicuously upon them anything that comes to hand. This system of occupation by proxy refers, however, more especially to the first class. With the majority of travellers by second and third class this delicate intimation does not appear to be understood, or, if understood, not recognized. In such cases it would be necessary to place some article of size and bulk in the place where you wish to sit, as a portmanteau or box, which some persons would be too timid, and others too idle, to remove. But where there is a party of some three or four, one of the company should see after the luggage and tickets, while the others sit wide, and thus retain between them a seat for their absent companion. If a person finds that he will not be able to arrive at the station until the very last moment, he should send his servant, or some one upon whom he could depend, to procure the ticket, retain the seat, etc. And if he have any business to transact, such as the posting of the railway accident insurance ticket, he should retain his seat at the earliest possible moment to afford ample time for the performance. Under any circumstances the number of the carriage and its position should be noted; otherwise, and especially if the *gage de séance* has been removed or accidentally displaced, the "unseated member" will be rushing from carriage to carriage in a state of bewilderment, and will be at last compelled to settle down anywhere, and take the chance of regaining his missing articles either during or at the close of the journey. Supposing you to have companions in the waiting-room, you will, after having selected seats for them, hasten to where you have left them, and escort them to the train; and this being off your mind, you will be enabled to see to the stowing away of the luggage—if this be not already done—or to perform any other office you desire. Occasionally an ill-bred person is to be met with, who will unceremoniously remove articles from a seat, disputing the right of pre-occupation, and appropriating the coveted place to himself. Such persons should be mildly remonstrated with, and if this fail, then an appeal should be made to the station-master or the guard, who will possibly be able to prevail upon the usurper to abdicate. But if he still persists in holding out, avoid anything like collision (ominous term on railways!), leave him to triumph in an ungentlemanly action, and seek a place in some

other portion of the train. We hold that altercations under such circumstances are not only useless, but unpleasant in their results. Here is an example:—
"Excuse me, sir, but you have taken my seat."
"Your seat, sir! nothing of the kind. Possession is nine points of the law, and you see I have it." "But, sir, I placed my travelling bag upon the seat ten minutes since." "And supposing you did, what then?" "What then! why, sir, you surely cannot be ignorant of the custom among railway travellers of securing seats by depositing articles upon them."
"I recognize no such custom; when I find a seat with nobody on it, I take it. I have taken this; and I mean to keep it." "Well, sir, all I can say is that you are no gentleman." "Perhaps not, sir; and on that account I should advise you to be civil." "What, sir, do you dare to threaten me? What do you mean?" "Pooh! pooh! don't bother me; go away and sit down." "But I'll let you know, sir, that——"
At this moment the familiar face of the guard appears at the carriage window, the door is closed, the whistle is blown, and the train starts, the claimant of the appropriated seat is obliged to find another where best he can, and the antagonists perform the journey either in open conflict, by talking at each other, or by silently looking daggers drawn, to the amusement, the annoyance, or both, of the other passengers, but to the decided chagrin, humiliation, and discomfort of him who has been worsted in the contest. We may perhaps be allowed to put in a word in favour of this custom of retaining seats. We consider, then, that there is nothing unfair in it, inasmuch as the oppor-

tunity is open to all, and on the universally recognized principle of "first come, first served," the
earliest comers at a station are certainly entitled to a
choice of places.   The book, the bag, the newspaper,
or other representative article ought to be respected,
for this shows (or at least in nine instances out ten)
that the person himself has been there, and it is somewhat exacting on the part of others to require a traveller to coop himself up in a close station a quarter
of an hour previous to starting, in order that he may
the more effectually defend his right against ill-bred
and wrong-headed pretenders.   When a train passes
through the station from which the railway traveller
departs, it is obviously impossible for him to retain a
seat, unless some sort of influence be brought to bear
upon the station-master or the guard in charge of the
train, or the good offices of some friend or acquaintance at the starting-point are put into requisition.
Nevertheless, we would advise the intending traveller
to take up his station on the platform, in such a position as will enable him to observe the interior of the
carriages as they flit by him, so that when the train
pulls up, he will be enabled if not to fix upon a particular seat, at least to select a carriage that is not
overcrowded, or the occupants of which appear most
congenial to his desires.   We also suggest that a
person thus waiting for a train to pass through, should
post himself on the platform a few yards in advance
of the station, and not absolutely within it, for it is
here that the crowd mostly congregate, and from
this point a certain amount of squeezing and hustling
is brought to bear, which it is as well to avoid.   Also,

generally speaking, the engine and foremost portion of the train shoots beyond the station, so that a person placed as we have indicated may take his seat leisurely and quietly in a half-filled carriage, while persons lower down are struggling to possess the vacant seats of carriages already over-crowded.

PROCURING TICKET.

The place where the tickets are issued is usually not open until within about a quarter of an hour of the departure of the train. Supposing, therefore, a passenger to have arrived at the station previously, he can employ the interval in looking after his luggage, selecting his seat, etc., and thus have nothing to attend to but the procuring his ticket. This process is usually so well managed that there is little crowding or confusion, each person taking his turn in regular order. In this comparatively trifling matter, as in every other, there is a right way and a wrong way of proceeding. All preliminary words are not only a waste of time, but quite unnecessary; the clerk sits at the counter for the purpose of ascertaining the place you are bound for, the class you wish to travel by, and the nature of the journey, whether single or double. The readiest way, therefore, of making yourself understood, is to apply for your ticket somewhat after this manner, "Bath—first-class—return," or whatever it may be.

We have previously alluded to the necessity of having a supply of change, and this applies with especial force to the procuring of the ticket. If you

know what the fare is, have the exact amount ready
in your hand, and if you do not know it, have the
money so handy that you may make up the sum without hesitation. By doing this you will not only
save your own time, but that of your neighbour.
Perhaps some of our readers may be able to call to
mind some such scene as the following, which is,
indeed, one of the incidents of almost every departing train : An elderly lady presents herself at the
ticket-counter, and expresses a wish to go to some
place at a short distance, say Putney. She first of all
inquires what is the fare first, second, and third
class ; upon being told that, she hesitates a few
seconds, and then thinks she will travel first-class.
Being asked whether she requires a single or return-
ticket, she appears to be astounded at the proposition,
ejaculates, " Eh! oh! ah!" at wide intervals, and
finally decides upon a single ticket, giving at the
same time her reasons for doing so. Having been
informed that the fare is ninepence, she dives for
her purse into some apparently unfathomable chasm
connected with her dress, and after considerable
rummaging, accompanied by a gingling of keys and
the production in succession of a pocket-handker-
chief, smelling-bottle, a pair of mittens, spectacle-case,
a fan, and an Abernethy biscuit, she at length suc-
ceeds in drawing forth an article which resembles an
attenuated eel. Thrusting her long bony fingers into
this receptacle, she draws out what she conceives to
be a shilling, but on nearer inspection she discovers
it to be a sovereign. She makes another dive and produces a half-crown, as she supposes, but this proves

to be only a penny-piece : finally, she manages to fish out sixpence, and connecting this with the penny-piece, and vaguely wondering whether she can find twopence more to make up the required amount, but without arriving at any satisfactory conclusion, she is at length constrained to give over further search, and to lay down the sovereign. Upon receiving her change, she examines each piece leisurely to ascertain if it be genuine; satisfied on this point, she counts her change over, repeating the process some four or five times, and on each occasion arriving at a different result. At length she makes out the matter to her satisfaction, then having carefully stowed away her change in such a manner that the first pickpocket may abstract it, she looks about her to see that she has left nothing behind, and after remarking how wonderfully the clerk resembles her nephew who has gone to the Indies, she somewhat reluctantly makes way for the next person. This is no overcharged picture, and we have no doubt that every one of our readers has in his time had his patience tried by some obstructive old lady bound for Putney or elsewhere. When you have received your ticket, put it in some place where it is not likely to be disturbed, but where it may be readily lighted on. If you deposit it in a pocket with other articles the chances are that in withdrawing any of these, the ticket may bear them company, and so be lost. This is a serious affair, since the ticket is a voucher that the traveller has paid his fare, and its non-production at the end of the journey entails the necessity of paying a second time. When you receive your ticket, ascertain that it is correct as regards the place you have booked for, the class you wish to travel by, and whether it be single or return; any error of this kind discovered immediately is soon rectified, but if allowed to pass, it cannot be so easily remedied afterwards, if at all.

Elderly or infirm persons, to avoid the inconvenience attending the procuring of the ticket, should ask one of the porters to perform that office for them, or prevail upon some person to obtain the ticket at the same time they do their own. When there are several persons belonging to the same party, one person will be sufficient to secure the tickets for the whole. Children under twelve years of age travel at half-price; when an adult, therefore, takes a ticket for himself and child. he asks for a " ticket and a-half ;" for every additional child under the limited age calculating a half-ticket. Persons should be cautioned not to tamper with the tickets in any way, and especially not to make use of or purchase passes which are not transferable ; the detection of these irregularities is productive of the most awkward and humiliating consequences.

SIGNAL FOR STARTING.

About five minutes before a train starts a bell is rung as a signal to the passengers to *prepare* for starting. Persons unaccustomed to travel by railway connect the ringing of the bell with the instant departure of the train, and it is most amusing to watch the novices running helter-skelter along the platform, tumbling over everything and everybody in their eagerness to catch the train which they believe is about to go without them. At the same time the seasoned traveller, who understands the intention of the bell, stands by the carriage door coolly surveying the panic-stricken multitude, or walks leisurely along the platform with the consciousness of being in ample time. The signal for the actual starting of the train is a whistle sounded by the guard, and when that is heard the journey commences in earnest.

ON THE JOURNEY.

SETTLING DOWN.

THE carriage and seat selected, all that has now to be done is to dispose yourself and your hand-luggage as comfortably and conveniently as possible. Any travelling bags, hat-cases, or small parcels which you take into the carriage with you, you will, of course, place beneath and above the seat at the point where you are sitting. It need be scarcely suggested that these arrangements should be made so as to inconvenience your fellow-passengers as little as possible.

STOWING AWAY HAND-LUGGAGE.

In placing articles in the net-work above the seats of the first-class carriages, care should be taken to lodge them securely, otherwise the motion of the carriage is apt to shake them from their position. We were once travelling in a carriage opposite to a lady and gentleman, above whose heads was a large square bonnet-box, a very small portion of which rested against the back of the carriage, and the remainder tilted over the edge in a most dangerous and threatening manner. After having our nerves excited to the very highest degree by the continual motion of the box and its imminent chance of falling, we took

the liberty of calling the attention of the gentleman
to it; but instead of expressing his thanks or remedy-
ing the defect, he tossed his head in a most offensive
manner, as much as to say, "Impertinent fellow!
mind your own business." Finding this to be the
case, we removed our seat to another part of the carriage, and we had scarcely done so, when down came
the box upon the heads of those immediately beneath.
The lady and gentleman sharing the damages between
them; the bonnet which the lady had on her head
was crushed and torn in such a manner as to render
her quite a figure; as for the gentleman, we failed
to catch sight of his expressive countenance for an
interval of at least two minutes, inasmuch as the box
had completely forced his hat over his eyes, nose, and
chin, and he had to make use of frantic efforts to
release his interesting features from their mask. And
when he did succeed in freeing himself his whole air
was so woe-begone, and his hat so battered as to
cause him to present a most woful appearance.
True, no blood was spilt, and no bones broken; but
both lady and gentleman were terribly frightened,
much shaken, and visited apparently with some afflic-
tion of the brain, which rendered them gloomy and
cross for the remainder of the journey.

MATERIALS FOR COMFORT—RUG, CAP, AND CUSHION.

If the season be cold, you will of course be provided with a railway rug. Before sitting down, wrap
this securely round your legs, and sit upon it so

as to keep it in its place. A rug is certainly one of the greatest comforts of a railway traveller, and none should be without it. Not only does it keep the legs warm, but on emergencies it may be made to perform the part of a cloak, a counterpane, a cushion to sit upon, or a wrapper for fragile articles. When it is not required it is very little in the way, and if neatly rolled up, and confined by a strap, may be easily transported from place to place with the other luggage without entailing much extra weight or bulk. Another mode of increasing the comfort of travelling is to have something to rest the feet upon, as a travelling bag, a small portmanteau, large parcel, etc. By this arrangement, not only is the draught from underneath the carriage-door avoided, but the lower portion of the body is more rested by this elevation of the legs. When the journey is a long one, and undertaken by night, great comfort will be found in a cap made to fit the head, and with lappets to draw over the ears. Having no projecting edges, the head may be thus leant back, without pain to the head itself or injury to its covering. The cold night air is also effectually excluded, and those painful visitants known as tooth-ache, ear-ache, and face-ache receive their *congé*. If the carriage travelled in be a second or third class, the hardness of the seats may be considerably modified by the use of an air-cushion; which, when not in use, is simply a roll of caoutchouc, but when inflated for use has all the appearance and effectiveness of an ordinary cushion. A species of green or black spectacles, known as eye-preservers, are excellent things for a railway traveller to carry with him, for if he be compelled to sit near the window, and opposite to the engine, he will find that by wearing these, the eyes will be preserved from the dust and ashes which are ever and anon intruding, and from the draughts of cold air which rush in at the window.

A person in a railway carriage may be likened to a prisoner of state, who is permitted to indulge in any relaxation and amusement to while away the time, but is denied that essential ingredient to human happiness, personal liberty. He is, in fact, confined to a certain space for so many hours, and cannot well remove from his allotted durance without annoying his fellow-passengers. The materials for railway amusement and relaxation embrace conversation, reading, card-playing, chess-playing, smoking, musing, and sleeping.

CONVERSATION.

With regard to conversation, the English are notoriously deficient in this art. Generally speaking, the occupants of a railway carriage perform the whole of the journey in silence; but if one passenger be more loquaciously inclined than the rest, he is soon silenced by abrupt or tart replies, or by a species of grunt expressive of dissent or dissatisfaction. Sometimes a conversation is got up, but it is of a spasmodic and ephemeral nature, lasts for about the first five minutes of the journey, and then relapses into solemn silence, never again to be broken. This is most unnatural and unreasonable. Why should half a dozen persons, each with minds to think, and tongues to express those thoughts, sit looking at each other mumchance, as though they were afraid of employing the faculty of speech? Why should an Englishman ever be like a ghost, in not speaking until he is spoken to? Some fanciful philosophers have asserted that monkeys might speak if they chose, only they are fearful that if they did, they would be compelled to work. This is not an Englishman's case, for surely he works hard enough, and has no penalty to escape. However, supposing Englishmen to so far forget themselves as to engage in conversation, let us insert a few words of advice on this head. Firstly, do not engage in discussions either political or theological; there is no knowing what tender chord may be touched, or what pain we may give to others in maintaining some pet theory or dogma. Besides, the utter inutility of all argument of this nature is notorious. Two men will argue for hours, each strong in his own opinion, and each bringing forward what he conceives to be irrefragable proofs of the soundness of his doctrine, and yet at the termination of the discussion, each disputant, in ninety-nine cases out of a hundred, is not only unshaken in his opinion, but clings to it more firmly than if he had never heard the other side of the case put at all. Besides, in conducting arguments of this kind there is sometimes danger of unwittingly working mischief to ourselves which we may afterwards repent. Here is a case in point: Two gentlemen, sitting opposite each other in a railway carriage, got into political argument; one was elderly and a stanch Conservative, the other was young and an ultra-Radical. It may be readily conceived that as the argument went on, the abuse became fast and furious; all sorts of unpleasant phrases and epithets were bandied about, personalities were freely indulged in, and the other passengers were absolutely compelled to interfere to prevent a *fracas*. At the end of the journey, the disputants parted in mutual disgust, and looking unutterable things. It so happened that the young man had a letter of introduction to an influential person in the neighbourhood respecting a legal appointment which was then vacant, which the young man desired to obtain, and which the elderly gentleman had the power to secure. The young petitioner, first going to his hotel, and making himself presentable, sallied forth on his errand. He reached the noble mansion of the person to whom his letter of introduction was addressed, was ushered into an ante-room, and there awaited with mingled hope and fear the all-important interview. After a few minutes the door opened, and, oh horrible to relate! he who entered was the young man's travelling opponent, and thus the antagonists of an hour since stood face to face. The confusion and humiliation on the one side, and the hauteur and coldness on the other, may be readily imagined. Sir Edward C——, however—for such he was—although he instantly recognized his recent antagonist, was too well-bred to make any allusion to the transaction. He took the letter of introduction in silence, read it, folded it up, and returned it to the presenter with a bitter smile, and the following speech: "Sir, I am infinitely obliged to my friend Mr. —— for recommending to my notice a gentleman whom he conceives to be so well fitted for the vacant post as yourself; but permit me to say that inasmuch as the office you are desirous to fill exists upon a purely Conservative tenure, and can only be appropriately administered by a person of Conservative tendency, I could not think of doing such violence to your *well-known* political principles as to recommend you for the post in question." With these words, and another smile more grim than before, Sir Edward C—— bowed the chapfallen petitioner out, and he quickly took his way to the railway station, secretly vowing never again to enter into political argument with an unknown railway traveller.

Another inappropriate theme of railway conversation is, any accident that may chance to have occurred recently. We have watched the countenancee, and observed the movements of old ladies, when listening to some graphic description of a railway accident which occurred only last week. We have expected those elderly matrons to faint every moment, and we have heard a suppressed groan or a faint shriek, when the train has bounced over a point, and given some idea to the uninitiated of something being amiss. Be it also observed, that unless it is otherwise mutually desired, the acquaintance begotten in the railway carriage ceases with the journey, and although you may have conversed as freely with a person as though you had known him twenty years, you would not be justified in accosting him in the street subsequently. We insert this little item of railway etiquette, because it may perchance prove useful, and without wishing to tire the reader, illustrate the position by the following incident :—

Lord B——, a member of one of the oldest families of the aristocracy, and Mr. G——, a London tradesman, happened to meet at the little island of Sark. The amusements of that remote and sea-girt place are few, and the number of visitors extremely limited. Thus these two men, although by birth, education, and habits, totally opposed to each other, were drawn into the bonds of association from a species of necessity. They boated, they fished, and they shot together. They dined at the same table, and took wine out of the same decanter; in short, for the whole period of their residence on the island, their several movements were a source of interest to each other, and they were seldom alone. When their time of stay was up, they travelled to London together, and at the terminus bade each other farewell. But poor G—— was somewhat chagrined by his lordship's manner, which perceptibly cooled as they neared the metropolis, and although he pressed Lord B—— over and over again to come and see him at his villa at Clapton, Lord B—— neither responded to the invitation, nor did he invite his *quondam* companion in return.

Some months rolled on, and the London season became at its height, when one day Mr. G——, walking down Bond Street, espied, on the opposite side of the way, Lord B—— coming along between two aristocratic-looking companions. Delighted at the idea of being able to show to the passers-by what a high-bred connection he could boast of, G—— crossed over and familiarly accosted his lordship, proffering his hand, and making kind inquiries as to the state of his health. But Lord B——, instead of appreciating these marks of friendship, drew himself up to his full height, and gazing intently through his glass, exclaimed, " Aw—to what happy circumstance am I indebted for the honour of your recognition ? Weally, I have not the pleasure of knowing you." "Not know me ?" shouted the astonished and outraged London tradesman. " Why, surely, my lord, you cannot have forgotten the pleasant time you and I had of it at Sark, last summer—my name is G——." " Oh, ah, Mr. G——; Sark—yes," responded his lordship. " Well, I have some faint recollection of something of the kind, and *if ever we should meet at Sark again, I shall be happy to renew our acquaintance.*" So saying, his lordship bowed and passed on, leaving poor G—— to reflections not very pleasant, on the instability of human friendship in general, and that of noble lords in particular.

READING.

Reading is an exhaustless fund of recreation. Ample provision is made on every book-stall along the line, of literature in every variety of form, so that " he who rails may read." It is always as well to provide one's self with a book or a newspaper, for if it is not used, you know you possess it, and can at any time fly to it by way of relief. It also forms an excellent weapon of defence against bores, that impertinent, intrusive, and inquisitive race, who can only be silenced by levelling a volume or a journal at their heads. If two or three persons in the same carriage purchase a newspaper, it is not a bad plan for each to select a different one, so that one may be exchanged for the other, and a variety of information obtained for the same outlay.

In selecting a book for railway reading, care should be taken that the type is large and clear, otherwise the eyes are tried too severely to do them any good. When reading in a railway carriage, the printed lines are apt to present the curious appearance of running into one another, and utterly defeating all attempts at perusal. One of the best means of preventing this is to place a strip of card just two or three lines below the one which is being read, and gradually move it down the page as perusal progresses. Reading at night by the aid of the ordinary railway lamp is a task difficult, if not impossible, to accomplish. A lamp has been invented which obviates this difficulty. It is of small size, readily lighted, extinguished, and trimmed, and furnished with a reflector which throws the light on the page. The lamp may of course be used for other than the special purpose for which it is constructed, and thus in more ways than one prove serviceable to the railway traveller.

It has been asserted that reading when travelling by railway proves injurious to the sight, and so it may be like everything else when carried to excess, and the reader will soon be warned of this by pain and weariness in the eyes. Certain it is, that out of every train that starts of two hundred passengers, one hundred at least may be noticed perusing a book or newspaper, and we are not aware of the existence of any national ophthalmic disease.

Let us now point out the best method of reading in railway carriages. In order to prevent the vibration of the carriages to the arms and book, do not rest the elbows on solid parts of the carriage, but hold the book or paper in both hands, and support it by muscular power. The arms thus disposed will impart an elasticity and *aplomb* to the volume, while the head, by being balanced on the neck, or at least not pressed or rested against the solid sides of the compartment, is equally free from communicating vibration to the frame.

CHESS-PLAYING AND CARD-PLAYING.

Chess-playing is a pleasant contrivance for whiling away the tedium of the journey, with those who are fond of the diversion. But the danger is in becoming too much absorbed in the game, as in the case of two players who intended to alight at Bath, but travelled on to Exeter. Card-playing, although somewhat difficult of accomplishment, is a pleasant pastime among friends, but beware of entering into this amusement with strangers. It is well known that a class of swindlers, known as card-sharpers, exist, who live by travelling in railway carriages and taking in the unwary. When, therefore, you are pressed to take a hand, or to select a card, or play a part in the performance of some sleight-of-hand business, have nothing to do with it; you are sure to be swindled out of your money, and have no remedy.

SMOKING.

Although smoking is prohibited ordinarily upon railways, some lines have certain smoking carriages provided, where the enjoyment may be indulged in without giving offence to others; he, therefore, who is inconsolable on the journey in the absence of his beloved weed, should take care to acquaint himself with the fact whether there are smoking carriages or not. We believe that on certain occasions the stringency of the prohibition is relaxed, and we were once present at the arrival of a train from Doncaster, during race-time, which train had more the odour of a divan than anything else, and every other passenger who alighted therefrom, held between his lips a partially consumed cigar.

MUSING, Etc.

Railway travelling affords a favourable opportunity for musing and reflecting, combined with that delightful occupation known as "building castles in the air." Trivial as it may appear, we yet think it worth recording, that the noise made by the train in its journey will accommodate itself to any tune, whether lively or sad, so that if a passenger choose to hum any of his favourite airs, he will find an accompaniment ready made.

Another source of amusement is reckoning the distance performed with the time occupied in the performance. To ascertain the distance travelled, the posts and gradients placed along the line must be

observed; these are situated at intervals of a quarter
of a mile from each other. Those on the left-hand
side to the country show the mileage from the metropolis; those on the right-hand side, the distance from
the provincial terminus.

SLEEP.

Sleep, the last resource of the tired and the weary,
readily visits the eyes of some railway travellers, while
to others it comes not, woo it as they may. The
head reclines, the lids are closed, the body is disposed
in the most favourable manner, but the attempt to
obtain slumber is totally unsuccessful. Some persons,
on the other hand, appear to sleep as well in the compartment of a railway carriage as they would on their
own domestic couch. We were once travelling by
the mail-train from London to Manchester; the train
was on the point of starting, and we had made up our
mind that we should have to perform the journey
alone. At that moment a tall bulky person entered,
and without looking either to the right or left, made
for the further corner of the carriage. By the aid of
a portmanteau and sundry packages he raised a structure between the two seats of the same height as the
seats themselves. He then swathed his body with a
capacious shepherd's plaid; after that he removed his
hat, and placed on his head a cap which fitted close to
the skull and came down over the ears; then he took
his seat, or rather assumed a recumbent position
across the two seats, and finally he tucked himself
with sundry rugs, and so fell asleep. From that mo-

ment we saw nothing more of our fellow-traveller than the tip of his nose; from that moment we heard no other sound than a bassoon-like accompaniment to the rattling of the train, in fact, a continuous and sustained snore.

When we arrived within a few miles of Manchester, the sleeper awoke as if by instinct, shook himself together, removed his rugs and plaid and cap, collected his parcels, and looked at us. We hereupon ventured to remark that he had had a nice nap, to which he replied that he always made a practice of enjoying his night's rest on the railway, and whenever it was practicable he preferred travelling by night, firstly, because he thereby gained time; secondly, because he thereby saved the expense of a bed at an hotel; and thirdly, because he stood one chance the less of being crippled or killed by the agency of a pair of damp sheets. We then ventured to ask what secret means he employed to insure such an uninterrupted slumber such as we had witnessed. He stared at us for a few seconds in astonishment, and then said, " Sir, *I make up my mind to it;* and let me tell you that it is as easy to make up your mind and to sleep, accordingly, as it is to determine upon eating your dinner, and to eat it. Halloo! here we are." With these words he cut short the colloquy, gathered up his packages and vanished. We set this remarkable man down as a travelling member of a philosophical society, or a political economist at least; but we afterwards learned that he was the representative of a highly respectable " button house."

Binns, in his entertaining work on sleep, gives a

recipe by which sleep may be procured at will, and which is somewhat to the following effect:—Dispose yourself comfortably on your right side, and place your hand beneath your head, shut your eyes, take a long inspiration, and then exhale the breath gradually, repeat this several times, and all the time you are doing so, imagine that you see a spiral wreath of smoke ascending towards the ceiling; if you can abstract your mind effectually, and continue it for a few minutes, you will fall asleep. This extraordinary plan has been adopted, it appears, by many persons of eminence, and has been approved by them. Another method of producing sleep is to close the eyes and repeat some simple piece of poetry, or count a certain number, say from 1 to 1000.

We mention these matters here, because a few hours' sleep frequently prove a great boon to the railway traveller, and if we can suggest any method by which that boon may be secured, these lines will not have been written in vain.

REFRESHMENT.

On a long journey refreshment will be needed, and this can be either obtained on the road, or the traveller may be his own purveyor, and take it with him. The rule generally is for the train to stop five or ten minutes for the purpose of taking refreshment; in such cases, especially with anything like a heavy train, a rush of passengers is made simultaneously towards the refreshment-room, and the counter is besieged by hungry and thirsty applicants, urging their various requests for sandwiches, buns, biscuits, wine, brandy, ale, etc. But inasmuch as there are usually some two or three hundred persons requiring refreshments, and only about a dozen hands to supply them, it stands to reason that the task of serving out the viands is no easy one, and many are the disappointments accordingly. Let the traveller remember that he has only the short space of five or ten minutes to gain the refreshment counter, to obtain the refreshment, to pay and perhaps receive change, to perform the operation of eating and drinking, and regain the seat in the carriage. It is obvious, therefore, that a person must exercise his utmost ingenuity and energy in order to accomplish this edible feat. Now, in this, as in everything else, a certain amount of tact is necessary to insure the desired end. When the train is on the point of stopping, mark well the place where the words "Refreshment-Room" are written up, so that directly the train stops, you may make at once for this place without wasting your time in looking about for it. Walk straight to that part of the counter where one of the attendants is stationed, and having, in parliamentary phraseology, "caught her eye," declare your wants. But in doing this, be quick and concise. If you desire a basin of soup, never mind the words "a basin of," but simply utter the monosyllable "soup;" so with a cup of tea, content yourself with calling out the latter word; a bottle of ale, "ale," etc. Call out distinctly and in a loud voice, have the precise sum ready, if you know what it will be, or at any rate tender a small coin.

Beware of taking hot refreshments; whether it be

by accident or design we know not, but certainly the fluids supplied are so excessively hot, and so long in forthcoming, that it is utterly impossible for a person to swallow them, unless his throat be sheathed with iron. Observe, also, that you should repair to the refreshment-room either immediately the train stops, or just before it starts again, for during the mid-interval the counter is literally besieged with a crowd of eager applicants, and a person standing behind these and endeavouring to make his wants known through the din of voices and the clatter of plates and cups and saucers, has but a very indifferent chance. On the whole, we should advise the railway traveller to take his refreshment with him; a few ham and beef sandwiches, together with a little cold wine or brandy and water will answer every purpose. And by this means a double advantage will be secured, for a person may partake of his refreshment at any moment he pleases, without being obliged to eat and drink at a particular moment dictated by the railway company; he will also obtain his refreshment at a much more moderate charge, and, further, he will have the interval to stretch his legs in, and to breathe a little fresh air, which he will find far more advantageous than being huddled and pushed about amidst a hungry and impatient crowd.

Every person who is about to travel a long distance, and is desirous of setting out with a feeling of comfort and satisfaction, should take care to provide suitably for the wants of the "inner man." And this is especially to be observed if the hour of departure be early in the morning, and that morning a cold and raw one. In the ordinary course of life every one recognizes the advisability of "laying a good foundation," as it is familiarly termed, or, in other words, making a breakfast so hearty and substantial as shall not only afford nourishment to the frame for some hours, but shall form an appropriate basis for the various kinds of sustenance introduced into the stomach during the subsequent portions of the day. This is a precaution which railway travellers neglect more than any other. The coming journey produces with many persons a state of nervousness and anxiety which deprives them of their appetite, so that after swallowing two or three mouthfuls of food, and half a cup of tea, they quit the table, and with this meagre provision they start for the station. By the time a few miles of the journey are accomplished, the appetite recovers itself, and the slighted repast is recalled to the mind with feelings of regret and vain desire. Under such circumstances, persons should force themselves to make a vigorous attack on the viands, and as, according to the French proverb, " the appetite comes in eating," the meal commenced with indifference may be continued with relish, and ended with gratification. At whatever time of the day the journey is to be accomplished, the traveller will be doing a wise thing to take some refreshment just previous to starting.

MARKING CARRIAGE FOR RECOGNITION.

When you leave a carriage during the journey, it is essential that you should be able to recognize it again on the instant. To facilitate this, every carriage door has the number placed on the inside of it, but although this assists a person to find his carriage, it is not all that is required. We suggest that a rug or shawl of red, or some other conspicuous colour, should be thrown across the carriage door, so that it may be seen at the distance, and may be at once regained without rushing from carriage to carriage to ascertain the number, or to take mental photographs of the passengers.

CHANGING CARRIAGES.

If the carriage in which you are is from any cause uncomfortable, you should get out of it at the first station, and enter another. This is sometimes absolutely necessary owing to the misconduct of other passengers, and it is infinitely better to leave them to themselves than to attempt to argue the matter with them.

If you wish to change from an inferior to a superior class, the plan is to speak to the guard, and he will have your ticket changed at the station, and the excess of fare will be charged for from the new starting-point; but if you change your class without consulting the guard, you will be charged the excess of fare for the whole journey. While we are upon this subject, we may observe that persons are sometimes placed by the railway servants in a superior class carriage, when they have a ticket for an inferior one. In such a case it will be well to direct the attention of the occupants of the carriage to the fact, so that you may be spared the annoyance and the overcharge which will be asked for on arriving at the terminus.

CARE OF RAILWAY TICKET.

The railway ticket should be guarded with care, as it is demanded at the end of the journey, and those who cannot produce it are compelled to pay again. It is useless to asseverate that you have paid and have lost your ticket. Such an assertion will not be heeded in the least; the simple fact of your not being able to produce it is regarded as the most certain sign of your not having paid, and therefore pay you must. A ticket may be also demanded during any part of the journey. The object, therefore, is to have it always safe and always handy; a portemonnaie, or pocket-book, is perhaps the best receptacle, or the inside of the left-hand glove; the worst place is certainly the pocket, where money and other things are ordinarily kept, on withdrawing which the ticket may be withdrawn too, and thus be lost.

LOOKING OUT FOR STATION.

If it is your intention to alight at some intermediate station, you must keep a sharp look-out to prevent being carried beyond it. Observe that the name of the station appears just before you reach it, and just after you pass it; not at the station itself. When a train is about to stop, there is a perceptible lessening of speed, so that it is always easy enough to direct your eye to the left side of the line, and note the name of the station. True, the porters sometimes call out the name of the place, but this they do so hurriedly, and in such a curious and varied dialect, that it is next to impossible to gather their meaning. For instance, when the train stops at Rochdale, you will hear the name called out as Rachdal, Rushdal, Roochdal, Rouchdal, and anything but what accords with your preconceived notion of the pronunciation of the name of the place. And thus it is with numerous other places, the name being pronounced in accordance with the *patois* of the place itself, and not agreeably to the rules of Walker.

VENTILATION AND DRAUGHTS.

In regulating the atmosphere of the railway carriage, the two main objects, of course, are to secure good ventilation, and to prevent draughts. This is easily done in first-class carriages, but not so easily in the inferior classes. The doors of the carriages are usually fitted with a sort of slide which may be closed or opened as occasion demands, and which in winter-time will be found to admit sufficient air without necessitating the opening of the window. But in summer-time, when it is considered necessary to open the windows, one only should be opened, and the one opposite the quarter in which the wind blows; the opening of both windows occasions a draught, which even in the warmest weather is apt to give persons colds, sore throats, stiff necks, etc. In passing through tunnels the windows should always be closed, as the air there is of the worst description.

When persons will insist upon having both windows down, the best plan is to leave that carriage and enter another; but if this cannot be done, then keep the head, throat, and mouth covered, the only measures that can well be taken.

CAUTION AGAINST LOOKING OUT OF WINDOW.

Some persons, when travelling by railway, have a knack of continually thrusting their heads out of window. Nothing can be more dangerous than this, and numerous are the accidents that have resulted in consequence. The proper place for the head is inside, not outside the carriage, and so long as it is kept there, the chances are that it will remain whole.

CAUTION AGAINST STANDING BY THE DOOR.

Children of all ages are frequently suffered by their parents to lounge against the door, which, if not properly fastened, is liable to give way to the pressure, and hurl the child foremost on the rails. Generally speaking, the door is fastened securely, but occasionally it is not, and this happening occasionally is sufficient evidence of insecurity.

CAUTION IN PASSING THROUGH TUNNELS.

Male passengers have sometimes been assaulted and robbed, and females insulted, in passing through tunnels. And this has been most frequently the case when there have been only two occupants in the carriage. In going through a tunnel, therefore, it is always as well to have the hands and arms ready disposed for defence, so that in the event of an attack, the assailant may be instantly beaten back or restrained.

ASKING INFORMATION.

When a railway traveller wishes to glean any information, he should not be afraid of asking his fellow-passengers. Among the occupants of the carriage there is sure to be at least one person who can answer the question put, and persons from whom information is sought usually feel complimented rather than annoyed. And yet there are persons of that reticent disposition who would rather run the risk of passing the station they desire to alight at, than ask any one respecting it.

BRANCH LINES AND JUNCTIONS.

When a traveller sets out for a place which involves a change of carriage at a branch line or junction, he should take care previous to starting to ascertain all about it; and, when the branch line or junction is arrived at, must exercise great caution in order to avoid getting on to the wrong line, and not enter a carriage without first making sure that he is right.

CROSSING THE RAILS.

When in passing from the up to the down station, or *vice versâ*, it is obligatory to cross the rails, it should be done with the utmost caution. Sometimes the order is not to cross the line unless accompanied by one of the company's servants. On other lines, persons are absolutely forbidden to cross the rails, and are directed to pass by the bridge erected close by. These injunctions should be obeyed in each instance. It touches one's *amour propre* to be called to account before a crowd of persons, while the passing over the bridge does not involve much labour, and is frequently more than repaid by the view which this eminence affords of the surrounding country. It may sometimes happen for a person to be on the line when a train is approaching, and when death appears imminent; this is one of the most awful predicaments which a human being can be placed in. In such a case the strongest brain may reel, and the stoutest heart quail. The men who work upon the railroad, and especially in tunnels, ordinarily adopt what may appear a most startling alternative to escape danger. When a train comes suddenly upon them, and does not allow of sufficient time to escape by flight, they are in the habit of throwing themselves flat on the ground, in the space between the up line and down line. Two trains have been known to pass a man in this position without injuring him in the slightest degree. But this requires great presence of mind, or rather that species of confidence inspired by known immunity from danger. The least motion to the right or the left, or upwards, might bring about certain and immediate death. The men who adopt this expedient are duly impressed with this fact, and while the engine and train are rattling over their heads with a fearful din, they lie as still as a child asleep in its cradle. There is another consideration for a person who finds himself in dangerous proximity of a train when crossing the line. Waterton, the celebrated traveller, in his "Wanderings," gives a graphic account of an escape from a boa constrictor, the gist of which is, that a person if he wishes to make good his retreat under such circumstances, should, instead of running straight forward, merely step on one aside, and the end is achieved. On the same principle, if in the majority of instances when threatened to be run down by an approaching train, the person in danger were to step backwards, instead of making forwards, fatal consequences would frequently be avoided. We were once witnesses of a most melancholy occurrence of this kind. A working man with a basket of tools slung over his shoulder, suddenly jumped from the up platform, and before any one could stop him was half across the line; at this moment a train suddenly darted round an adjacent curve on the down line, and was coming onwards at full speed. It may be imagined that the greatest excitement prevailed among the persons on each side of the platform, and various and conflicting were the directions shouted from every mouth. The poor fellow in a state of bewilderment, and quite unconscious of what he was doing, made a forward movement, but before he could clear the rails, the train was upon him, and a fearful groan and a mangled mass but too truly told the story. Now, if instead of hastening forwards, the poor fellow had made a retrograde motion of only a yard, he could have accomplished it in far less time, and would have been entirely removed from danger. As a general injunction it should be laid down that no one should attempt to pass the line if a train be in sight. The eye is apt to be greatly deceived in the distance, and the relative pace at which the train is travelling. And even under the most favourable circumstances, a person knowing the danger he is running, is apt to become nervous and irresolute; his foot may slip at the most critical juncture, and he may be thus hurled prostrate across the line, and be unable to recover himself, before the train has performed its mission of destruction.

ENTERING AND LEAVING THE CARRIAGE WHILE IN MOTION.

Numerous accidents have arisen to railway travellers from their folly in persisting to enter or leave a carriage while in motion. There is an express law against this, and the misdemeanour is punished with a fine of forty shillings, which, in addition to any personal injury that may have been sustained, is paying rather dearly for one's obstinacy. At the end of a journey everybody is naturally anxious to quit the train as soon as possible, and hence the impatience manifested, and the foolish leaps made. Few persons are experienced in the rate of railway travelling, and when the train is moving at the rate of twenty miles an hour, it appears not to be travelling faster than five or six miles an hour, and with this miscalculation it is easy to understand that a false step may be made, and the body thrown off its equilibrium.

H

After all, the time saved in getting out of the train before it absolutely stops, is about the tenth part of a minute. If any person near you should be rash enough to attempt leaving the train before it stops, do not try to prevent him; for being thus baulked, he is almost sure to stumble, and the consequences may be fearful.

UP LINE AND DOWN LINE.

In nautical language the terms "starboard" and "larboard" are employed to express the right and left sides of the ship. And among whips, "off side" and "near side" are used to denote the same relative positions. The custom with regard to the latter has been well expressed in the following verse:—

> "The rule of the road is a paradox quite,
>   As you'll find when you're driving along;
> If you keep to the left you are sure to be right,
>   And if you go right, you go wrong."

In accordance with this principle, the trains in their onward progress invariably keep on the left side of the line, the passengers getting in and out on the same side. The word "up" signifies towards London, or any other large city or important terminus. The term "down" means from London, etc., to provincial towns or places of lesser note. These words are so familiar to the ears of railway officials, that when a person is asking information respecting the trains, he must adopt these technicalities if he desires to make himself intelligible. This up and down business is apt to bewilder inexperienced and unthinking persons

If they alight at a station on one side of the line, they cannot understand why, when departing from the station, they have to cross to the other side. We have already pointed out why this is so, and, therefore, when a person is about to return to the place whence he came, he must look out for the sign-post, which is generally near, pointing to the up trains, or the down trains, as the case may be. For if he have but a few minutes to spare, and goes to the wrong station, the chances are that while he is running round to the other, the train will be off.

RAILWAY SIGNALS.

A knowledge of the meaning and intention of the various signals may, in many cases, prove useful to the railway traveller. There are three principal signals in use, which are shown differently by day and night—"*Danger*," to stop ; "*Caution*," to go slowly ; "*All right*," to go on. FIXED SIGNALS are placed at stations, tunnels, junctions, level crossings, and other places where caution is required. FIXED DAY SIGNALS.—*Danger, to stop*, is shown by turning the cross bar of the mast signal full upon the line, so that it can be well seen from the approaching train, and by a red board pointing to the rails. *Caution, to go slowly*, is shown by a green board pointing from the rails. *All right, to go on*, is shown by turning the disc of the mast signal full upon the line, so that it can be well seen from the approaching train. FIXED NIGHT SIGNALS.—*Danger, to stop*, is shown by a red ight fixed upon a pole being turned full upon the line, so that it can be seen from the approaching train. *Caution, to go slowly*, is shown in the same manner by a green light. *All right, to go on*, is shown in the same way by a white light. Post Signals.—The signal posts are furnished with two arms, one moving out on one side to give signals to trains on the down line of rails, and another moving out on the other side of the signal post to give signals on the up line of rails. The signal is invariably made on the left-hand side of the post, as seen by the approaching engine-driver. The position of the arm on the right-hand side is consequently a signal to trains running in a contrary direction. The *all right* signal is shown by the left-hand side of the signal post, as seen by an approaching engine-driver, being clear. The *caution* signal, to *slacken speed*, is shown by the arm on the left-hand side being raised half way to the horizontal position. The *danger signal, to stop*, is shown by the arm on the left-hand side being raised to the horizontal position; when both arms are raised both lines are blocked. Flag Signals.—When the line is clear, and nothing to impede the progress of the train, the policeman, or other person on duty, stands erect with a white flag in his hand. If it be necessary to proceed with caution, from another engine having passed on the same line within ten minutes, a green flag is selected and held towards the approaching train. If there be any defect in the rails, the green flag is depressed, the points touching the ground. If required to stop, the red flag is shown and waved to and fro. Hand Signals, by Day.—*Danger, to stop*, is shown by raising both arms above the head. *Caution, to go slowly*, is shown by holding the right arm above the head. *All right, to go on,* is shown by extending the arm straight out, and pointing across the rails. HAND SIGNALS BY NIGHT are made by hand lamps with different coloured lights, thus: *Danger, to stop,* by a red light shown steadily towards the approaching train. *Caution, to go slowly,* by a green light held towards the train. *All right, to go on,* by a white light held towards the train. WHISTLE SIGNALS.—On approaching each station and level crossing, and on entering a tunnel, the engine-driver gives one long whistle. Two short whistles denote that the engine-driver considers caution necessary, and is a signal for the guard to be on the outlook. Three short, sharp whistles denote that danger is apprehended, and is a signal for the guards instantly to put on the breaks.

SIGNALLING GUARD IN EMERGENCIES.

The difficulty of communicating with the guard of a train is one of those defects in railway management which cannot apparently be overcome. But on emergencies, signals can be improvised by a passenger in a carriage, sufficiently conspicuous to arrest the attention of the guard. It may be necessary to do this in the event of the carriage catching fire, a passenger being taken ill, or any other emergency, and the best plan is to tie a coloured handkerchief on to the end of a stick, and hold it out as far beyond the carriage as possible. But will the guard understand this and stop the train accordingly? We think he will, and are led to suppose so from the following incident:—

We were once in a carriage with a farmer, who, on passing a village, took out his handkerchief and waved it to and fro several times to some person seated at the window of a house; this signalling lasted several seconds, and in a short time the train stopped, and the guard came to the carriage to know if anything was amiss. The matter was soon explained, and the guard pointed out that had he not stopped the train, and had there been anything amiss, he should have considered that he had been guilty of culpable neglect.

HOW TO ACT IN CASES OF THREATENED ACCIDENTS.

Presence of mind is essentially demanded in all the accidents of life, but in none more so than accidents by railway. Also, when accidents are imminent, but do not actually occur, coolness and judgment are necessary. When the train comes to a sudden standstill at an unaccustomed stopping-place, it is usually a sign that there is something amiss; but this something may be of very trivial moment. At all events, do not vex yourself with the idea incessantly that catastrophes are about to occur, nor pester the guard with questions only to receive ambiguous and evasive replies. If an absolute stoppage takes place, the best plan is to quit the carriage, and then whatever may occur you will be safe. In cases where the carriages are felt to be overturning, there is but one method, and that is to jump from the upper side as the carriages go over, and in taking this jump the feet should be placed close together, the arms held close to the side, and the body inclined forwards.

Many concussions give no warning of their approach, while others do, the usually premonitory symptoms being a kind of bouncing or leaping of the train. It is well to know that the bottom of the carriage is the safest place, and therefore, when a person has reason to anticipate a concussion, he should, without hesitation, throw himself on the floor of the carriage. It was by this means that Lord Guillamore saved his own life and that of his fellow-passengers some years since, when a concussion took place on one of the Irish railways. His lordship feeling a shock, which he knew was the forerunner of a concussion, without more ado, sprang upon the two persons sitting opposite him, and dragged them with him to the bottom of the carriage; the astonished persons at first imagined that they had been set upon by a maniac, and commenced struggling for their liberty, but in a few seconds they but too well understood the nature of the case; the concussion came, and the upper part of the carriage in which Lord Guillamore and the other two persons were was shattered to pieces, while the floor was untouched, and thus left them lying in safety; while the other carriages of the train presented nothing but a ghastly spectacle of dead and wounded. If a person be buried among the *debris* of the carriages, and is still in possession of life and limb, he should endeavour to make his way out of his perilous position in an upward direction, and in the event of the windows being blocked up, force a passage in the best manner he can by the aid of a stick or umbrella. If the accident occur in an open part of the line, a person on escaping from the carriage should remove himself as far from the scene as possible, until all immediate danger is over, and he is permitted to return and assist his fellow-passengers in distress. If the accident occur in a tunnel, then a person should grope his way along by the side of the wall, feeling with his hand, and keeping his body as close to the brickwork as possible.

In numerous cases of concussion, severe and fatal wounds have been caused to the heads of passengers by the hard, sharp brim of the ordinary hat, which, when impelled forward, would appear to cut like a knife; this hint is worth attending to. On the same principle, it is obvious that the softer the body a person has to oppose, the greater are his chances of escape, and bearing this in mind, a seat in a first class carriage, opposite one that is unoccupied, is the safest, because the body is then opposed to the padded back of the carriage, and, under these circumstances, seldom sustains serious injury. Although it is perhaps easier to lay down rules of conduct in such cases than to follow them, yet the following incident will show that foresight and presence of mind, as in the case of Lord Guillamore, work to the greatest advantage:—In the terrible accident that occurred on the North London line, at Camden Town, one of the passengers at the moment of concussion spread out his arms and inclosed with them as many passengers as he could. A mass being thus welded together offered substantial resistance to the shock, and the whole of those persons escaped with only a few slight bruises, while others around them were killed or severely injured.

Railway accidents are rendered less terrible by the presence of lamps. On some lines the second and third classes are unprovided with lamps, but on all lines lamps are provided for first-class passengers; if, therefore, a person on entering a carriage find there is no lamp, he should call the attention of the guard to the omission, and insist on its being rectified previous to starting.

TREATMENT OF RAILWAY SERVANTS.

At every station there is an officer, termed a station-master, or superintendent, who has under his control all matters connected with both the passenger and goods traffic at that particular point of the line. To him all communications should be made in reference to any special arrangements that a person desires to make. To him, also, representations should be made of any irregularities, shortcomings, or neglect on the part of his subordinates. The porters at the various stations have to take charge of the luggage of passengers arriving and departing, and to render such other assistance as may be required. These porters are usually attired in a suit of dark-coloured corduroy, and will always be found in and about the station. When a passenger desires to have his luggage removed or conveyed from one place to another, he has only to mention his wish to one of these men, and it will be instantly attended to. In order to insure their prompt attention, care should be taken to address a porter who is disengaged, not one busied in loading or wheeling baggage, or otherwise obviously preoccupied. The guards are those men who are specially appointed to certain trains, and who have a train under their charge from the moment it commences taking in its freight of passengers and luggage, until it arrives and is cleared at the terminus. They usually wear a uniform of blue or green cloth, and are distinguished by a small whistle hanging at their breast The guard is the proper person to make inquiries of respecting the train previous to starting, or to prefer any complaints to during the journey. In addition to their strictly defined duties, they will undertake such other little offices on behalf of passengers or their friends as will not interfere with the usual routine.

Every railway servant has a distinctive number affixed either to the collar of his coat or to his cap, so that when a complaint is made of any of them, this number should be stated. All representations of misconduct or neglect of duty, which are made in writing, should bear the name and address of the accuser. An anonymous communication only serves to raise a vague kind of prejudice against the accused person, while it is inoperative in redressing the particular grievance to which attention is called. While we are on this point we think it right to impress upon the railway traveller how essential it is that he should be not only charitable but circumspect in preferring complaints. Some persons are exacting, and require too much to be done; others are hasty, and demand prompt attention to their desires; others again are captious, and imagine rudeness and incivility where none has been intended. Added to these special fault-finders, there are a number of grumblers and objectors who are continually giving vent to incoherent utterances depreciatory of all persons and all things. As a rule, the various railway *employés* are civil, intelligent, and obliging, and in this spirit any request courteously and distinctly made will be duly responded to. All railway servants are strictly prohibited from taking any fee or reward, and persons who act in contravention of this wholesome regulation lay the foundation of an incalculable amount of mischief. Another foolish custom is the treating the guards with drink while on the journey; this is usually done, from ostentatious motives, by those who consider it a fine thing to take railway guards under their patronage in the matter of brandy-and-water. To such a mischievous extent was this pernicious custom carried on a certain railway, that a terrible accident was clearly traceable to the inebriety of the person in charge of the train, and the inebriety was occasioned by drink with which he had been plied by some of the passengers in the course of the journey.

ECONOMY IN COMPANIONSHIP.

Individual charges are considerably lessened when they are divided between two or more persons. A cab or fly for two is little more expensive than for one. The same candles and firing will equally as well serve a company as a solitary individual. Two persons may call for a pint of wine between them at an hotel without being considered mean; whereas one person ordering half a pint would be regarded as stingy. A double-bedded room is much cheaper in proportion than two single ones, especially if accommodation be scarce; and so on through the whole catalogue of travelling charges. From these remarks it is obvious, that, where practicable, it is not only a great saving, but considerably more pleasant to travel in company than alone. But companions are sometimes not ready-made. We saw an advertisement in the *Times* a short time since, where a gentleman advertised for another to accompany him to the Continent, on the share and share alike principle. And although we do not counsel the cultivation of acquaintanceship with strangers except with the utmost discretion, yet, from a casual meeting on the road, many companionships are undoubtedly formed which prove mutually advantageous and economical.

TREATMENT OF UNPLEASANT TRAVELLING COMPANIONS.

Railway travellers are occasionally thrown into company with persons who know not how to behave themselves, or rather those who consider it the height of manliness and propriety to insult inoffensive and quietly-disposed passengers. These monsters are especially fond of molesting females, well-knowing that for the time being the unfortunate objects of their persecution are in their absolute power. A few words

decidedly and firmly addressed to such individuals
will sometimes have the desired effect, but this only
seldom. Another method is to lodge a complaint to
the guard, and insist on the offender being removed;
but inasmuch as the officials frequently exhibit great
tenderness on behalf of the culprit, and are apt to
imagine that the other passengers are over-squeamish,
the guard usually contents himself with administer-
ing a few words of mild reproof, without attempting
removal. A case of this kind once occurred on the
Eastern Counties line. A big hulking fellow, with
bully written on his face, took his seat in a second-
class carriage, and forthwith commenced insulting
everybody by his words and gestures. He was asked
to desist, but only responded with language more
abusive. The guard was then appealed to, who told
him to mind what he was about, shut the door, and
cried, " all right." Thus encouraged, the miscreant
continued his disgraceful conduct, and became every
moment more outrageous. In one part of the carriage there were four farmers sitting who all came
from the same neighbourhood, and to whom every part
along the line was well known. One of these wrote
on a slip of paper these words, " Let us souse him in
Chuckley Slough." This paper was handed from one
to the other, and each nodded assent. Now, Chuckley
Slough was a pond near one of the railway stations,
not very deep, but the waters of which were black,
muddy, and somewhat repellant to the olfactory nerves.
The station was neared and arrived at; in the meantime Bully's conduct became worse and worse. As they
emerged from the station, one of the farmers aforesaid

said to the fellow, "Now, will you be quiet?" "No, I won't," was the answer. "You won't, won't you?" asked a second farmer. "You are determined you won't?" inquired a third. "You are certain you won't?" asked the fourth. To all of which queries the response was in negatives, with certain inelegant expletives added thereto. "Then," said the four farmers speaking as one man, and rising in a body, "out you go." So saying, they seized the giant frame of the wretch, who struggled hard to escape but to no purpose; they forced him to the window, and while the train was still travelling at a slow pace, and Chuckley Slough appeared to view, they without more ado thrust the huge carcass through the window, and propelling it forward with some force, landed it exactly in the centre of the black filthy slough. The mingled cries and oaths of the man were something fearful to hear; his attempts at extrication and incessant slipping still deeper in the mire, something ludicrous to witness; all the passengers watched him with feelings of gratified revenge, and the last that was seen of him was a huge black mass, having no traces of humanity about it, crawling up the bank in a state of utter prostration. In this instance the remedy was rather a violent one; but less active measures had been found to fail, and there can be little doubt that this man took care ever afterwards not to run the risk of a similar punishment by indulging in conduct of a like nature. On starting for a journey, do not enter a carriage where you observe rough and noisy company, and if you are already seated, and a disorderly character attempts to enter, try to keep him out. There are other passengers who are not absolutely offensive, and yet disagreeable to travel with. There is the fidgetty traveller, who is continually shifting his body into every variety of position, and shuffling about his legs and feet without the slightest regard for the legs and feet of other people. The best plan is to remove from the vicinity of such irritating persons. Or if you cannot do that, a slightly angular projection of the knee or elbow may have a quieting effect. There is the inquisitive passenger, who wishes to know more respecting yourself than you care to reveal to a stranger. When you recognize such an individual, take up a book or newspaper, and commence an attentive perusal of it. If this will not answer the purpose, go off into a sound sleep, and respond to his interrogations by a loud snore. Then there is the prosy traveller, who inflicts upon you a series of narratives of most immaterial and inconsequential incidents which are neither interesting, amusing, nor enlightening; to such twaddlers you may appear to be attentively listening—that is all they require—while in reality your mind is busily occupied with affairs of real moment and interest. There is the staring traveller, who, in the rudest manner possible, deliberately fixes his eye upon you, and never removes it until he has scanned your person, features, and costume to his entire satisfaction. We said never removes his eye, but that is the case with timid persons and those of the softer sex, who feel abashed under the circumstances, and let fall their eyelids. The way to meet this piece of insolence and vulgarity is to return stare for stare, to fix your eye upon the offender at the same moment and in the same manner that he fixes it on you, and, our word for it, he will feel the reproof and withdraw from the contest. There are other classes of unpleasant travelling companions whose bare mention would only tend to needlessly burden these pages. Of whatever kind and degree, avoid them altogether if you can; if that be not possible, quit their company at the first opportunity; and if this be impracticable, bring your ingenuity and philosophy to bear to lighten the infliction.

BYE-LAWS AND REGULATIONS.

The several railway companies have powers and authorities vested in them by Act of Parliament, which passengers are bound to abide by. In some instances there are special rules made to meet exceptional circumstances; but the bye-laws and regulations, relating to passenger traffic generally on all the lines, are in substance as follows:—1. No passenger will be allowed to enter or travel in any carriage used on the railway without having first paid his fare, and obtained a ticket. Each passenger, on payment of his fare, will be furnished with a ticket, specifying the class of carriage, and the distance for which the fare has been paid; which ticket such passenger is to show when required by the guard in charge of the train, or other servant of the company duly authorized to take tickets, and to deliver up before leaving the company's premises. Any passenger not producing or delivering up his ticket, will be required to pay the fare from he place where the train originally started, or, in default of payment thereof, shall forfeit and pay a sum not exceeding forty shillings. 2. At the intermediate stations the fares will only be accepted, and the tickets furnished conditionally, that is to say, in case there shall be room for all the passengers to whom tickets have been furnished; those to whom tickets have been furnished for the longest distance shall have the preference, and those to whom tickets have been furnished for the same distance shall have priority according to the order in which the tickets have been furnished, as denoted by the consecutive numbers stamped upon them. 3. Any person travelling without permission, in a carriage of a superior class to that for which he has obtained a ticket, or attempting in any other manner to evade the payment of his full fare, is thereby subjected to a penalty not exceeding forty shillings. 4. Smoking tobacco is prohibited both in the carriages and in the company's stations. Every person so smoking is subjected to a penalty not exceeding forty shillings; and every person persisting therein after being warned to desist by any officer of the company, shall, in addition to incurring the aforesaid penalty, be immediately, or if travelling, at the first opportunity, removed from the company's premises. 5. Any person found in a carriage or station in a state of intoxication, or committing any nuisance, or otherwise wilfully interfering with the comfort of other passengers, is hereby subjected to a penalty not exceeding forty shillings, and shall be immediately, or if travelling, at the first opportunity, removed from the company's premises. 6. Any person cutting the lining, removing or defacing the

I

number-plates, breaking the windows, or otherwise wilfully damaging or injuring any carriage used on the railway, shall forfeit and pay a sum not exceeding five pounds, in addition to the amount of any damage for which he may be liable. 7. No passenger shall be permitted to ride on the roof, steps, or platform of any carriage; any person persisting in doing so, after being warned to desist by the guard in charge of the train, or any officer of the company, is hereby subjected to a penalty not exceeding forty shillings 8. Any passenger entering or leaving, or attempting to enter or leave any of the carriages, while the train is in motion, is hereby subjected to a penalty not exceeding forty shillings. 9. Dogs will not be suffered to accompany passengers, but will be conveyed separately, and charged for. 10. Any person who, having paid his fare for a certain distance, shall knowingly and wilfully proceed in any such carriage beyond such distance, without previously paying the additional fare for the additional distance, and with intent to avoid payment thereof, or who shall knowingly refuse or neglect, on arriving at the point to which he has paid his fare, to quit such carriage, is for every such offence liable to a penalty of forty shillings; and any person committing such offence may be lawfully apprehended and detained by the company's officers and servants, until he can be conveniently taken before some justice. 11. Persons wilfully obstructing or impeding the company's officers in the execution of their duty, are liable to be apprehended and fined five pounds, with two months' imprisonment in default of payment. 12. No fee or gratuity is permitted to be taken by any guard, porter, or other servant of the company, under pain of immediate dismissal.

PECULIAR REGULATIONS AND CHARACTERISTICS OF VARIOUS RAILWAYS.

French Railways.—In travelling by French railways all luggage has to be surrendered to the officials, and a fee of two sous paid for a ticket, which the holder has to give up at the end of his journey, to regain possession of his luggage. Sixty pounds of luggage is allowed free of charge, any excess of weight being charged for. On alighting from the train, at the end of the journey, the traveller has to proceed to the platform, where he will discover his luggage among that of others, he has then to give up his keys to the examining officer, and to receive a permission to pass. The examination of luggage is necessarily tedious and annoying, and a person wishing to escape it should leave the matter in the hands of his servant. If, however, you have determined upon staying at any particular hotel, you may, by pre-arrangement with the hotel-keeper, secure the services of a confidential person, who will be sent to meet you at the station, to take charge of your luggage, and bring it on to you at the hotel. If, by choice or necessity, the examination of the luggage falls personally upon you, and supposing you to be accompanied by a lady, the best arrangement you can make is to conduct her to a *fiacre* (cab) close by, there to wait until you rejoin her with the luggage.

German Railways.—The carriages on German railways are notably fitted up in a superior manner, and the second class so nearly approach the comforts of the first, that few persons travel by the latter. The fare of the second class is one-third or fourth less than that of the first. It is to be borne in mind, however, that smoking—that universal practice in Germany—finds its way into every second class carriage, and there is no way of escaping this but to ride by first class. Stringent regulations are in force on the German railways with regard to luggage; under the most favourable circumstances, forty pounds only are allowed free of charge, and even one pound over-weight is charged for as for one hundred pounds. On the Wurtemburg line ten pounds only is allowed; whilst on the Bremen railway all luggage must be paid for. Travellers carrying luggage should be at the departure station some time before the train starts, as the weighing, ticketing, and paying for luggage, is a very tedious process. Numbered tickets are affixed to every article, and a corresponding receipt is given to the owner, which he must produce at the end of his journey, in order to reclaim his property.

Austrian Railways.—Travelling by these is not so comfortable as in Northern Germany, the accommodation is indifferent, even of the first class. Here, also, the rules respecting luggage are very strict; forty pounds only are allowed, the remainder being charged for at a moderate rate.

Dutch Railways are generally well managed, liberally conducted, and comfortably appointed.

Belgian Railways.—A moderate rate of travelling, and a low scale of fares, are the most conspicuous features of the Belgian railways. The accommodation is, for first class passengers, luxurious. The second class is comfortable for males but not for females; one great objection being that in order to reach or quit one's place, the seats, owing to a paucity of doors, and a lack of convenient arrangement, have to be clambered over in the most awkward and indelicate fashion. The third class consists of waggons, open at the sides, and fitted up with wooden benches. On Belgian railways the arrival and departure of the trains is very badly managed, and the traveller will find it as much as he can do to avoid being carried away in the vortex of hurry, crush, and confusion. At certain points of the line the bewilderment is increased by the crossing of trains, the changing of carriages, and the removal of luggage. And the traveller will have to take especial precaution that he is not run over, or carried in a wrong direction. With regard to luggage, passengers are allowed to retain parcels which are not too large to go under the seats of the carriage, all larger articles are taken away, and conveyed as luggage proper. At this point we may appropriately throw out a few hints respecting the luggage of foreign travellers generally. From what has been just stated it will be gathered, that in order to save trouble, time, anxiety, and expense, the luggage should be reduced to the lightest possible weight, and the smallest practicable bulk. The best plan will be to have only a bag, which may be stowed away under the seat, or carried in the hand. It will thus be necessary to bestow some little pains and reflection on the process of packing up, selecting only those articles which are likely to be absolutely required, and rejecting such as in all probability would be carried from place to place, and finally brought home without having been once put in requisition. When a good deal of luggage is indispensable, it is a great mistake to distribute it into numerous small packages. Three large portmanteaus are infinitely better than six small ones, they are more readily recognized on arrival, more easily found at the Custom House, cost the same when charged by weight, and, of course, half as much when charged by package.

American Railways.—These present the very acmé of comfort and convenience. You can buy your railway ticket in the carriage ; and there you can have every convenience of a moving hostelry, excepting the actual meals. You can purchase a newspaper or a book to while away the time ; you can have a breath of fresh air on the platform outside the car ; you can have a bed at night ; in short, you might literally lodge in the train, without leaving it once, for days together. The pace, it is true, is slow comparatively with that adopted on English railways, but this is compensated for by the greater amount of convenience and comfort, and the less liability to accident.

LIABILITY AND NON-LIABILITY OF RAILWAY COMPANIES.

Railway companies render themselves liable to an action at law for compensation, when death or personal injury has resulted from an accident on the line. But in order to make good the claim, defect, mismanagement, or carelessness on the part of the railway direction or the railway servants must be proved. Where an accident has arisen from the carelessness or misconduct of the injured person, the company is clearly not liable. With regard to luggage and other effects, the company is professedly not liable for any loss, unless the value of such property has been declared, and booked and paid for accordingly. But this view of the case is susceptible of being considerably modified by special circumstances. For instance, a London jeweller was travelling by an Irish railway, having in his possession a jewel-case, containing property upwards of a thousand pounds in value. This case he took with him into the first-class carriage, and placed it beneath the seat he occupied. In the course of the journey he left the carriage for two or three minutes, and on his return he discovered the jewel-case to be gone. He immediately gave information of his loss to the station-master and others, but notwithstanding an instant and rigid search, no traces of the missing property could be discovered. A claim for compensation was subsequently sent into the company, but they declined to entertain it, on the ground that the owner of the property had not exercised reasonable care and diligence in the protection of his property. An action was brought against the company, and a verdict returned for the plaintiff, for it was held that he *had* exercised reasonable care and diligence ; the mere quitting of the train for two or three minutes (the main point of objection) was no contravention of the railway regulations, and the officers in charge of the train were held to be responsible for the property left in a carriage by a passenger while performing the journey.

The various railway companies do not bind themselves to the times of departure and arrival advertised by them. They undertake to use their best efforts to insure punctuality, but they disclaim any liability for the loss which a passenger may represent to have sustained by the delay. Some years since there prevailed a sort of passion for bringing actions against railway companies on this plea. A few successful verdicts for the plaintiff encouraged many unscrupulous persons to pursue the same course, and in some cases, speculative journeys were undertaken, with a view of fixing the company with the responsibility of delay. It accordingly soon became obvious that it would be impossible to answer claims of this nature, and hence railway companies were relieved of the *onus* which was sought to be cast upon them in this direction. There are numerous minor points of liability and non-liability, but they are not of sufficient importance to demand special mention.

AFTER THE JOURNEY.

COLLECTING BAGGAGE.

LET us now suppose the traveller arrived at his destination. We may premise that as he draws near to the terminus, he gathers together the various articles he has with him, so as to be able to emerge from the carriage immediately the train stops. We are anxious to lay some stress on this provision, because there are persons who neglect to take this precaution, and who at the last moment are to be seen rummaging beneath the seats, exclaiming, in half-stifled voices, " Dear me, I've lost my bag." "Where's my hat-case gone?" "I can't find my umbrella," and so on. What ought to be done is to collect the things together, and to consider whether you have all. Place these under your arm, in your hands, or otherwise conveniently dispose of them; if you are travelling in company let each bear his share of the burden. If your ticket has not been taken, be sure you have it handy and ready to deliver up.

MEETING FRIENDS.

If any friends are going to meet you at the station, do not increase their anxiety by putting your head out of the carriage window before the train stops, because as you must withdraw your head to allow other passengers to alight, your friend loses sight of you, and becomes confused in his search from one carriage to another. Keep your place quietly, let your fellow-travellers leave the carriage, and then show yourself at the carriage door, standing full in view, and conspicuous above the surrounding crowd. If you have appointed to meet some one to whom you are personally unknown, you should, by pre-arrangement, have some mark or sign by which you may instantly be recognized; a piece of ribbon in the button-hole, or a card inserted beneath the hatband will answer this purpose.

ENGAGING CAB, ETC.

If you wish to engage a cab or a fly, hand your bag or rug to one of the porters who comes to the door as the train enters the station, desiring him to engage you a cab, and noting his number, so that you may afterwards request him to point out the vehicle he has engaged. If you do not see a porter, then hail a cab from the rank drawn up in the station, keeping your eye upon the man you have engaged, and making straight for him directly you leave the carriage. It may here be observed that the drivers of four-wheeled cabs prefer persons with luggage to those without, as they can see a clearer prospect of profit, and the chances are that if you have only a small handbag, and walk down the rank, each driver in succession will tell you he is engaged, and you will therefore have wasted your time to no purpose. We should advise luggageless travellers to hail a "Hansom," that vehicle being a species of light cabillery, and setting up rather for speed than capacity. But perhaps the quickest way of all is to quit the station as speedily as possible, outside of which there will generally be found plenty of vehicles ready and eager for a job. If it be an omnibus you are going by, make towards it without a moment's hesitation, for the chances are that there will be more passengers wishing to go by it than it is able to accommodate.

DISPOSAL OF LADIES AND CHILDREN.

Should you be accompanied by ladies, by children, or by both, it is essential that you should remove them out of the noise, bustle, and confusion inseparably attendant on the arrival of a train. If the arrangements you have to make will occupy only two or three minutes, you may leave them in the carriage till you can rejoin them. If you are likely to be any length of time in completing your arrangements, then the best plan is to conduct your companions to the waiting-room, there to remain until you have done all you have to do. If you succeed in engaging a vehicle immediately on your arrival, and have nothing further to detain you, then you may at once conduct them to the vehicle, and afterwards see about your luggage.

LOOKING AFTER LUGGAGE.

As a matter of course, a railway traveller should, on reaching his destination, look after his luggage as speedily as possible. If the number and position of the van in which, or upon which the luggage has been placed, has been noted, as previously advised, then there will be no difficulty in finding it. As the luggage is delivered from the vans, porters are standing near to convey it to such place as the owner may direct. Directly you recognize your articles claim them, and ask one of the porters standing by to carry them for you. At such a juncture beware of thieves, who infest railways for the purpose of misappropriating luggage that is unclaimed, or claimed hesitatingly. Be cautious, also, that you yourself do not lay claim to luggage that is not your own. Many packages closely resemble each other, and in the hurry of the moment they may be confounded; but in nearly every case there is some distinctive feature perfectly familiar to the owner, and which he should look for to avoid error. It is an extremely awkward affair to be detected in the act of walking off with some other person's property, and although the mistake may be explained subsequently, it yet entails a considerable amount of mortification humiliation, and delay.

RECLAIMING LOST LUGGAGE.

Through the carelessness of passengers, luggage is frequently lost or mislaid, and it will be as well to know the best method of regaining such missing articles. In the first place, it should be known that when the train is emptied of its passengers one of the company's servants enters every carriage, lifts up the seat and the carpet, looks under the seats, and otherwise makes a careful inspection, and any articles found by him are forwarded to the terminus. Here, there is a lost luggage office, in which all stray property is received. A description of each article is entered in a book, stating the day, the time, etc., when found. If the articles inquired for are not traceable at the chief station, a description is sent to each of the offices where lost luggage is kept. If this application be unsuccessful, the superintendent applies to the manager of the Railway Clearing-house, who writes to all the stations on the various lines of railroad, and if it be at none of these stations, a letter is then addressed to the inquirer, informing him that his lost property is not on the railway. All unclaimed property is forwarded to the head station, and kept there pending inquiries made with a view to ascertain the addresses of the owners ; and if such addresses can be ascertained, the property is forwarded on the payment of a fine of 6d. for each article. If the property be not claimed within two years, it is sold by public auction. Obviously, therefore, what a person has to do when he misses any portion of his luggage, is to make such loss known immediately to the stationmaster, giving as correct and minute an account of the missing articles as he possibly can to facilitate inquiry. He should also charge his memory as to the last place where he saw his luggage safe. But in respect to these, we may mention a well-authenticated circumstance in connection with lost luggage, namely, that property is frequently not regained because persons are so positive that they have left it in such and such place, and therefore do not think it worth while to inquire at any other place. We see instances of this treachery of memory combined with overweening confidence in every-day life. Let all persons, therefore, take the hint, and be upon their guard accordingly. If a person has reason to think that his property has been taken in mistake or stolen, the best plan is to advertise instantly in the *Times*, and at the same time to put himself in communication with the police, who will materially assist his search. In all these cases delay is dangerous; active measures must be taken on the instant, for every lapsing moment renders the chance of recovery more remote. It should also be known that every cab which leaves a railway station has its number taken by a person stationed at the gate, together with the place to which he is engaged to drive. Thus, any traveller who may have left any property in a cab has only to state on which day and by what train he arrived, also whither he was conveyed, and from these data the driver's name and address can at any lapse of time be readily ascertained. But beside this, it is advisable that a person should take the number of the cab-driver previous to entering the cab, thus rendering the task of recovery easier still.

SENDING INTIMATION OF SAFE ARRIVAL.

When a railway traveller has left behind him those who are near and dear to him, it is but natural that they should be anxious to hear of the safe arrival of the " dear departed ;" and in such cases it is a great piece of cruelty to withhold that which may be so readily imparted. And yet it is common enough for a traveller to promise that he will write, but on his arrival to neglect to do so. *He* himself is perfectly conscious of his safety, and appears to think that others, however far removed, ought to be cognizant of the agreeable fact. When he gets to his hotel or lodgings, he pretends that he is too tired to write, that it will do very well to-morrow, and thus suffers those from whom he is separated to be in a state of the greatest anxiety for four-and-twenty hours. The remedy for this is simple enough. Let the railway traveller, just previous to starting, write a note headed with the name of the place to which he is going, and stating that he has arrived safely; this, put into an envelope ready addressed and stamped, the traveller can take with him, so that upon his arrival he has simply to post it, and the purpose is duly answered. Anything by way of postscript may be added in pencil, or if it is considered more genuine, the whole of the note may be written in pencil, and placed into the envelope prepared for it.

DESPATCHING TELEGRAPHIC MESSAGES.

At any time during the journey, or when he has arrived at its termination, the railway traveller may call to mind some important matter which he is desirous of communicating to those whom he has left behind. For such emergencies the telegraphic wires are ever ready to obey the behests of their employers ; and through their medium any error may be rectified, or any neglect repaired while the traveller continues his journey at his ease. Nearly every station has a telegraph office attached to it, so that all a traveller has to do is to write his message on a slip of paper, and at any station deliver it to the guard, together with the fee, and everything is then done.

HIRING PORTER.

If a person does not require a vehicle, he will seldom have any difficulty in finding a porter to carry his luggage. A crowd of men and boys are usually to be met with outside the terminus who, for a trifling fee, will convey the luggage to any part of the town. It would be as well to hire a clean and honest-looking messenger, and also to take the precaution of making him walk on in front, as you will then have your eye upon him, and he cannot well decamp without your knowledge. On the principle of seeking information from everybody, you may, while jogging onwards, glean from your luggage-bearer such items of intelligence as will prove advantageous.

LEAVING ARTICLES AT THE STATION.

It is sometimes of the utmost convenience to leave your luggage at the station while you settle any pre-liminaries incidental to an arrival in a fresh place. For instance, if you have not yet secured your lodg-ings, you will be able to do so much better without your luggage than with it. Or if you are going to stay at an hotel, you may select at your leisure the house at which you would prefer to stop, without being forced to put up at any particular hostelry, through the cajolery of the fly-driver and the pertinacity of the landlord. Frequently the fly-driving and hotel interest work into each other's hands, the fly-driver receiving from the landlord so much per head for every customer brought. When, therefore a person arrives at a town he has not hitherto visited, and places himself and his luggage in a fly, intent upon putting up at an hotel, but without any knowledge of which is the best, it is a common thing enough to appeal to the fly-driver, and he, as in duty bound, drives you straight off to his employer for the purpose of receiving his reward. It need scarcely be remarked that the proprietors of hotels who descend to this system of bribery have ordinarily not the best of houses, their larder and cellar being alike indifferent, and their accommodation execrable. But there are a variety of circumstances which render the leaving of luggage preferable to carrying it about. The stay in the place may only be a short one, perhaps not more than a few hours. When, therefore, the passenger arriving, wishes to leave his luggage, he should have it conveyed to the office set apart for that purpose, paying a small fee of some 2d. or 3d., and receiving a ticket in return. The production of the ticket will be sufficient to insure the delivery of the articles, so that the owner need not trouble to go for them himself if he does not feel so disposed.

FORWARDING PARCELS BY COMPANY'S EXPRESS.

At almost every terminus, parcels will be taken charge of and forwarded by what is termed the Company's Express, carts and other vehicles being employed for that purpose, and a great deal of trouble being thus taken off the hands of the traveller who is saddled with packages to be delivered at various places. The rates charged are moderate, and safety and speedy delivery are insured.

NOTING TIME OF DEPARTURE OF RETURN TRAINS.

When a person alights at a station, from which he intends returning the same day, he of course ought to know the times of departure. If he is not provided with a railway guide, this information will be gained on consulting the time-table which is usually hung up near the entrance of the station, and if there be no time-table, or there be any difficulty in understanding it, the necessary information may be obtained from the porter who takes the ticket at the gate. In such cases memory is not to be trusted, and a memorandum of the times should be taken.

NOTING THE POSITION OF THE STATION.

When a person is about to return to the station at which he alights, and will in all probability have to do so in a hurry, in order to catch the train that is passing through, he should observe the relative position of the station in connection with the other buildings by which it is surrounded, and the turnings right and left which lead from it to the town. So that on coming back, the station may be reached without difficulty without inquiring the way, which consumes time, and without going in a wrong direction, which is worse than all. Should the traveller be at a loss, let him look about him for the telegraph wires and posts, running his eye along these till he recognizes the top of the station, and then following up the clue.

REACHING ACROSS COUNTRY AND OUT-OF-THE-WAY PLACES.

A railway traveller is destined occasionally to alight at a station which is removed some seven, eight, or ten miles from the place he wishes to reach. Possibly no cab, fly, or omnibus is to be had; he cannot walk it; what then is he to do? The best plan in such a dilemma is to repair to the nearest inn, and make inquiries for any vehicle under a post-chaise and four. Generally speaking, the landlord has a pony and gig with which he goes to the nearest market, or a four-wheeled chaise that he drives his wife and daughters in to the next town. Or if he has not one, he knows some neighbour who has, and if it even be a tax-cart, it is preferable being conveyed by that, to passing the best part of the day in some dreary and desolate hamlet.

WHILING AWAY THE TIME AT STOPPING STATIONS.

It sometimes happens that a person has to wait the arrival of the train at the station of some little country town. Under such circumstances, time hangs most heavily, and an hour appears as long as a day. The amusements within reach are of the most meagre description. The two or three persons who wander in and out of the station may have no marked peculiarities, and they are but two or three after all. There may be a few cocks and hens in the adjacent poultry-yard, but they are probably lazy or replete, and their movements are of the most commonplace and uninteresting description. As to the town itself, the chances are that it has little worth seeing, and a peregrination of its utmost limits can be accomplished in ten minutes. To while away the time under such unpromising aspects is somewhat of an art. If a person have a book with him, he need look no further for recreation. If not, let him procure three or four sheets of writing paper, a pen, and a bottle of ink, bring them back to the waiting-room, and sit down to write two or three letters to as many friends. It is astonishing how quickly time flies with those who are using the pen. If the thoughts come with difficulty, then much time is consumed in bringing them to bear; if thoughts come readily, then the noting them down consumes time also. Another end is accomplished, since time is economized and put to a good use, which would be otherwise frittered away.

RATES OF TELEGRAMS.

The rates for forwarding telegraphic messages vary with the different railway companies; the following scale will, however, be found to approach the general charges as nearly as possible: For 25 miles, 1s., 50 miles 1s. 6d., beyond 50 miles 2s., for messages not exceeding 20 words. Half these rates are charged for every 10 words, or portion of 10 words, not exceeding 20 words. *Cypher communications* sent according to same rates, four cypher or private signals being considered equal to 20 words. Each word underlined, in Italics, or within parenthesis, or between inverted commas, will be counted and charged as two words. Messengers are despatched immediately on arrival of message. The charge, if within 3 miles, 6d. per mile on foot, or 1s. per mile by cab, horse, etc., if beyond 3 miles 1s. per mile by the readiest available means. No porterage is charged if the distance be within half a mile. For distances within 10 miles, if sent by rail only 6d. per mile is charged; and porterage in London is charged 6d. per mile for the first 3 miles, and 6d. for every half mile beyond 3 miles, 1s. per mile if by cab. As the charge for telegraphic messages is regulated by the number of words, it is obviously essential to make the message sent as concise as possible, pruning it of all redundant words and tautologies; but while aiming at brevity, care must be taken not to relapse into ambiguity, as illustrated by the following anecdote. The husband of a lady of rank, residing at Edinburgh, engaged the services of an eminent London practitioner for his wife's approaching accouchement. About the time the auspicious event was expected to occur, Dr. —— received the following message : "Don't come too late ;" and in obedience to this summons he immediately set out for the North. Arrived at the mansion, he was received by the husband with an air of astonishment, and an inquiry as to whether the telegraphic message had been received. Dr. —— replied that he certainly had received such message, and that was the immediate cause of his appearance in Edinburgh. " God bless me !" said the husband, " that is very extraordinary, for I should have thought the message would have had the effect of preventing your coming, as, indeed, was the intention, for, to tell you the truth, the little stranger had already come to light when the message was sent, and as that was the case, word was sent to you not to come, as it was too late." " Well," said the doctor, " you may have meant such a message to have reached me, but the one I received was, ' Don't come too late,' and thinking that the event was momentarily expected, I did not hesitate a moment to place myself in the train, and here I am." " I see it all," said the husband, " it is simply an error in punctuation, the message as sent being, ' *Don't come— too late*,' so that although the same words were transmitted, their meaning was widely different." Similar misunderstandings, equally as ludicrous as this, have occurred over and over again, arising, in nearly every case, from a want of explicitness.

ACCOMMODATION FOR RAILWAY TRAVELLERS.

A few words on this subject may prove useful. If you intend staying at an hotel, and are a stranger to the place, make inquiries among your friends as to which is the best house to stop at. Under any circumstances, never select a second or third-rate hotel, its accommodation is always inferior, and its charges usually exorbitant. If there exists the probability of an influx of visitors into the town, the precaution should be taken of pre-engaging a room by writing to the landlord a few days previously. Should the bustle and noise of an hotel be objected to, very good accommodation is to be met with at a boarding-house. If apartments are desired, and some difficulty is experienced in obtaining them, temporary quarters may be taken to afford time for looking out for the more permanent home. In some cases, neither hotel accommodation nor apartments are to be had. To remedy this want, a bed-room may be engaged at a private house, and the meals taken at an hotel. It should be borne in mind that where private apartments are occupied at an hotel, the charges are much dearer than when the ordinary accommodation of the coffee-room is accepted. The same remark applies to dinners, etc., specially ordered, instead of partaking of the fare provided for the common table. Some persons are desirous of securing the comforts of an hotel, without incurring the expense or the obligation of taking intoxicating liquors. To meet this view, many towns have what are termed Temperance

Hotels, where the desired end may be achieved. Finally, we would warn travellers that in many instances they will have to put up with discomfort, and they will rarely meet with all the comforts of a home. Instead of chafing at these drawbacks, the best way is to be prepared for them, to treat them as lightly as possible, and as the French say, " accept the situation."

Having thus brought the Railway Traveller to the end of his journey, and seen him safely housed, we cannot do better than devote the few remaining pages of this little volume to items of information which cannot fail to prove generally useful, and especially so to the excursionist and to visitors from the country.

EXCURSION GUIDE.

THE following is a list of places which may be readily reached by any of the railways, and to which excursion trains run throughout the season:—

BATH.—One of the most beautiful cities in England, containing many interesting buildings, and standing in the midst of exquisite scenery. Great Western Railway. Distance, $106\frac{3}{4}$ miles. Average time of journey, four hours.

BRIGHTON.—One of the most delightful places out of London at which to pass a day or a few days. The air is particularly bracing and enjoyable. The Downs afford the best walking and riding, and the sea-bathing is unequalled. Brighton and South Coast Railway. Distance, $50\frac{1}{2}$ miles. Average time of journey, two hours.

CAMBRIDGE.—Celebrated as the seat of one of our great English universities, and thus possessing considerable interest. The buildings in connection with the colleges are well worth seeing, and the country around is remarkably picturesque. Eastern Counties Railway. Distance, $57\frac{1}{2}$ miles. Average time of journey, two hours and a-half.

DEAL.—A small but interesting maritime town. Near it are situated Walmer and Sandown Castles. The air is extremely salubrious, and the coast affords extensive views of France and the Kentish shore. South Eastern Railway. Distance, 102 miles. Average time of journey, four hours.

DOVER.—Remarkable for its cliff, and for numerous interesting fortifications of various styles—Roman, Saxon, Norman, etc. The sea-bathing is excellent, and the town capable of affording superior accommodation to visitors. South Eastern Railway. Distance, 88 miles. Average time of journey, three hours.

EASTBOURNE.—A pretty little town in Sussex, situated close to the sea. Near this place is BEACHY HEAD, one of the finest marine eminences in England, and the prospect from which is very striking. Brighton and South Coast Railway. Distance, 66 miles. Average time of journey, two hours and a-half.

GRAVESEND.—A town in Kent, with an extensive river view, and possessing several interesting walks around it. On account of its easy access from London, it is greatly resorted to during the season. North Kent Railway, and London and Tilbury Railway. Distance, 23 miles. Average time of journey, one hour and a-half.

HAMPTON COURT.—An exceedingly interesting place, having a royal palace, picture gallery, and pleasure grounds. The walks in the neighbourhood are extremely pretty, especially that known as Bushy Park. South Western Railway. Distance, 15 miles. Average time of journey, three-quarters of an hour.

HASTINGS.—A town of great antiquity, pleasantly situated in a vale, and facing the sea. The country abounds with pleasant walks and drives, and the sea-bathing accommodation is of a superior description. Adjoining Hastings is St. Leonards-on-Sea, which has an air of quietude and retirement about it peculiarly agreeable to invalids. South Eastern Railway. Distance, 74 miles. Average time of journey, two hours and a-half.

Herne Bay.—A favourite watering-place, situated in a beautiful bay, commanding an extensive prospect of ocean, and much resorted to for the purpose of sea-bathing, and enjoying its peculiarly healthy and bracing air. South Eastern Railway. Distance, 84 miles. Average time of journey, three hours.

Kew.—Celebrated for its botanical gardens, which are said to be the most extensive in the world. The walks around are charming. South Western Railway. Distance, 9½ miles. Average time of journey, thirty-five minutes.

Lewes.—A place situated on the margin of the South Downs, surrounded by high hills, from one of which may be obtained a prospect of thirty miles to the sea and forty miles inland to Surrey. Brighton and South Coast Railway. Distance, 50 miles. Average time of journey, two hours.

Margate.—A favourite bathing-place, on the north coast of Kent. Its air is remarkably salubrious, and the town has a variety of amusements to set before the visitor, which render the place highly attractive. South Eastern Railway. Distance, 101 miles. Average time of journey, three hours and a-half.

Oxford.—The situation of this city is one of surpassing beauty. It stands between the rivers Isis and Cherwell, and is surrounded by hills of gentle elevation. The city itself is rich in classic associations, the university and various college buildings possessing great interest for the visitor. Great Western Railway. Distance, 63½ miles. Average time of journey, two hours and a-half.

PORTSMOUTH AND ISLE OF WIGHT.—The principal naval arsenal and fortress in England, possessing an unlimited amount of interest in connection with maritime affairs. Within a short sail of Portsmouth is the Isle of Wight, well known for its numerous beautiful spots, and celebrated for its excellent sea-bathing. South Western Railway, and Brighton and South Coast Railway. Distance, 74 miles. Average time of journey, three hours.

RAMSGATE.—A noted sea-bathing place, situated near Margate, and to which it is by many preferred, as being more retired and select. In addition to its excellent sea-bathing, there are some very pretty drives and walks in the neighbourhood, which render it on the whole, one of the most attractive places of resort. South Eastern Railway. Distance, 97 miles. Average time of journey, three hours and a-half.

READING.—A town of great antiquity, pleasantly situated on the river Kennet. It has many architectural features, which render it highly interesting. It also abounds in charming walks and drives. South Western Railway (36 miles), Great Western Railway and South Eastern Railway (67 miles).

RICHMOND.—One of the most beautiful spots near the metropolis. The park is of a gently-undulating character, enriched by pieces of ornamental water, and is between eight and nine miles in circumference.

The hill affords a magnificent and extensive prospect, and the scenery immediately at its foot is of unrivalled beauty. South Western Railway. Distance, 9¾ miles. Average time of journey, forty minutes.

RYE HOUSE.—A popular resort for summer excursionists, and on account of the beauty of the gardens, and the various recreations provided for the visitors, few places are better adapted for a day's excursion. There are historical associations connected with Rye House which render it still more interesting. Eastern Counties Railway. Distance, 20¾ miles. Average time of journey, one hour.

SALISBURY.—One of the most interesting cathedral towns of England. The sacred edifice itself presents one of the finest and most interesting specimens of Gothic architecture in the kingdom; and the buildings by which this magnificent and venerable pile is surrounded, are in keeping with the structure itself. In the immediate neighbourhood there are several mansions of noble proportions, and also a ruin of the palace of the great Clarendon. South Western Railway. Distance, 83¼ miles. Average time of journey, four hours.

SOUTHAMPTON.—A large and pleasant town situated on the banks of a broad expanse of water rendered particularly interesting by the assemblage of shipping, and other incidents of maritime traffic. The walks in the neighbourhood are varied and very beautiful. It also possesses many architectural features, and is especially celebrated for one of the most picturesque ruins in England, known as Netley

Abbey. Altogether, the mildness and salubrity of the air, the beauty of its position, and the picturesqueness of its scenery, render this town a delightful place of resort. South Western Railway. Distance, 79 miles. Average time of journey, three hours.

SOUTHEND.—A small but improving town, pleasantly situated on the Essex coast, and especially eligible for the Londoner, as being the nearest point from the metropolis where sea-bathing can be had. It has a pier stretching a mile and a-quarter in length, and is noted for the very pretty walks in the immediate locality. There is an air of calm and quiet about this little place, which renders it especially suitable for the debilitated frame, and the harassed mind. London and Tilbury Railway. Distance, 42½ miles. Average time of journey, two hours and a-quarter.

VIRGINIA WATER.—A very picturesque spot in the neighbourhood of Windsor. It is chiefly remarkable for a large sheet of artificial water, the cascade of which affords one of the most striking imitations of the great works of Nature; the grounds by which it is surrounded are arranged upon the most imposing style of landscape gardening. South Western Railway. Distance, 23 miles. Average time of journey, one hour.

WEYMOUTH.—A watering-place, once extremely fashionable, and still much resorted to. It is pleasantly situated in a delightful bay of the English Channel. The esplanade is a feature of great beauty, and is nearly a mile long. The gradually shelving shore especially adapts it for sea-bathing. The air is remarkable for its mildness and purity. South Western Railway. Distance 147¼ miles. Average time of journey, six hours.

WINCHESTER.—A fine old city, rich in its associations with English History, and still retaining the remains of former greatness. It is beautifully situated in the midst of swelling downs, and a river runs through the valley hard by. The architectural beauties are numerous, including Butter Cross, the County Hall, Wolverley Palace, William of Wykeham's College, etc., all of which are well worthy of especial notice. South Western Railway. Distance 66½ miles. Average time of journey, two hours and a-half.

WINDSOR.—A town deriving its chief importance from its being a favourite residence of the English monarchs. The Castle is famed for its architectural beauty; and from the cliff on which it stands, a most magnificent and extensive prospect is to be obtained. The adjacent parks are beautifully laid out, and the College of Eton, on the outskirts of the town, will well repay a visit. South Western Railway. Distance, 25½ miles. Average time of journey, one hour and a-quarter.

WORTHING.—A pretty and retired watering-place in the vicinity of Brighton. It is remarkable for the mildness of its air; and, owing to its sheltered position, for the facilities which it affords of sea-bathing, even in the winter months and in stormy weather. Brighton and South-Coast Railway. Distance, 61 miles. Average time of journey, two hours and a-half.

EXHIBITIONS (Admission on Payment.)

BURFORD'S PANORAMA, LEICESTER SQUARE.—A large picture of Naples, together with views of Messina, Straits of Faro, the Court of Venice, Rome, Calabria, Switzerland, etc. Open daily. Admission 1s.

COLOSSEUM, REGENT'S PARK.—A variety of entertainments and exhibitions, including Dioramas of London, Paris, and Lisbon. Open daily—morning twelve; evening, seven. Admission 1s.

CRYSTAL PALACE, SYDENHAM.—A variety of entertainments and exhibitions, including pictures, statuary, flowers, fountains, performances by an orchestral band and on the great organ, together with special amusements according to the season of the year. Open daily. Monday, nine; other days, ten. Admission:—Saturday, 2s. 6d.; other days, 1s. Children half-price. Sunday, open at half-past one to shareholders, gratuitously by tickets.

KENSINGTON EDUCATIONAL MUSEUM, SOUTH KENSINGTON.—Works of decorative art, modern pictures, sculpture, and engravings; architectural illustrations, building materials, educational apparatus and books, illustrations of food and animal products. Open every day in the week. The Museum is open free on Monday, Tuesday, and Saturday. The students' days are Wednesday, Thursday, and Friday, when the public are admitted on the payment of 6d. each person. The hours on Monday, Tuesday, and Wednesday are from ten till four; on Thursday, Friday, and Saturday, from ten till four, five, and six, according to the season.

POLYTECHNIC, REGENT STREET.—Musical entertainments, lectures, chemical and other experiments, dissolving views, etc. Open daily. Morning at twelve; evening at seven. Admission 1s.

MADAME TUSSAUD'S WAXWORK.—A collection of life-like representations, modelled in wax and appropriately dressed, of numerous eminent and notorious personages, together with relics of Napoleon, Wellington, etc. Open daily. Morning, ten; evening, seven. Admission 1s.

TOWER OF LONDON.—The principal objects of interest are the Chapel of St. John, the Council Chamber, the White Tower, the Armoury, and the Regalia. Tickets to be obtained at the entrance. A warder is in attendance every half-hour to conduct parties in waiting. Admission to the Armouries, 6d., and to the Crown Jewels, 6d. Open daily, from half-past ten to four.

ZOOLOGICAL GARDENS, REGENT'S PARK.—Containing a large and valuable collection of wild and domesticated animals. The gardens are extensive and are beautifully and tastefully laid out. Open daily. Admission, 1s.; Mondays, 6d.

EXHIBITIONS AND PLACES OF INTEREST.

(ADMISSION FREE.)

BANK OF ENGLAND.—From nine in the morning until three in the afternoon (except holidays), when strangers are at liberty to walk through.

BOTANICAL GARDENS (CHELSEA).—May be seen by tickets, obtainable at Apothecaries' Hall, Water Lane, Blackfriars.

BRITISH MUSEUM.—Open to the public on Mondays, Wednesdays, and Fridays; daily during the weeks of Easter, Whitsuntide, and Christmas; and on Saturdays in the summer months after twelve o'clock. It is closed during the first week of January, May, and September.

BUCKINGHAM PALACE.—To be viewed only by special favour, and generally through the interest of some person connected with the Royal Household.

CHELSEA HOSPITAL.—An asylum for disabled and superannuated soldiers. The chapel may be seen for a trifling fee to the pensioner in charge of it, any day except during Divine Service, on Sundays, Wednesdays, and Fridays. The Great Hall may also be seen when not in use. Admittance to the grounds from ten till dusk, except during Divine Service on Sunday morning.

CHRIST'S HOSPITAL, OR BLUECOAT SCHOOL, NEWGATE STREET.—Maintaining upwards of 1000 children. Admission by ticket, obtainable at the office attached to the school.

COAL EXCHANGE, LOWER THAMES STREET.—Public admitted free to the Museum on the first Monday in each month, from twelve till four.

COLLEGE OF SURGEONS, LINCOLN'S INN FIELDS.—Contains the collection of the celebrated anatomist, John Hunter. Admission by member's ticket on Mondays, Tuesdays, Wednesdays, and Thursdays, from twelve till four.

DULWICH GALLERY, DULWICH, SURREY.—About four miles from London. Comprises a splendid collection of pictures and other objects of interest. Open daily, from ten till five.

GEOLOGICAL MUSEUM, JERMYN STREET, REGENT STREET.—Open every day (Fridays excepted).

GREENWICH HOSPITAL, GREENWICH, KENT.— About five miles from London; accessible by rail or boat from London Bridge. The Painted Hall is open from about nine in the morning till dusk. Free after twelve o'clock, and by payment of 4*d.* before that hour. On public holidays free the whole day.

GRESHAM COLLEGE, BASINGHALL STREET, CITY. —Lectures on various subjects at various seasons of the year.

GUILDHALL, KING STREET, CHEAPSIDE.—Public Hall open daily. The apartments to be seen by applying to the hall-keeper.

HAMPTON COURT.—A magnificent palace with gardens attached, situate at Hampton, fifteen miles from London, and accessible by steamboat and railway. The State apartments, containing a large collection of pictures, are open every day except Friday, from ten till six. On Sundays after two.

HOUSES OF PARLIAMENT.—May be viewed on Saturdays from ten till four, by tickets to be obtained at the Lord Chamberlain's office within the building. The Victoria Tower on Saturdays.

INDIA MUSEUM, WHITEHALL YARD, PARLIAMENT STREET.—Open on Mondays, Wednesdays, and Fridays, from ten till four.

KEW GARDENS.—One of the most extensive and

interesting horticultural exhibitions in the country Open from one till dusk. Sundays after two. May be reached by rail, omnibus, or steamboat.

NATIONAL GALLERY, TRAFALGAR SQUARE.—Open on Mondays, Tuesdays, Wednesdays, and Saturdays.

NATIONAL PORTRAIT GALLERY, 29, GREAT GEORGE STREET, WESTMINSTER.—Wednesdays and Saturdays, from twelve till four, between Michaelmas and Easter; from Easter to Michaelmas, from twelve to five.

ROYAL BOTANIC SOCIETY'S GARDENS, REGENT'S PARK.—Admission by tickets from members.

ROYAL MINT, TOWER HILL.—Admission by order from the Master's office, Little Tower Hill.

ST. PAUL'S CATHEDRAL.—Admission within the sacred edifice free; to the whispering gallery and the two outside galleries, 6d.; to the ball, 1s. 6d.; to the library, great bell, and geometrical staircase and model rooms, 6d.; to the clock and the crypt, 6d.

SIR JOHN SOANE'S MUSEUM, LINCOLN'S INN FIELDS.—Open every Thursday and Friday in April, May, and June. Cards of admission on written application to the Curator at the museum.

SOCIETY OF ARTS, JOHN STREET, ADELPHI.— By member's ticket. Daily, except Mondays and Wednesdays.

THAMES TUNNEL.—Best accessible by boat from London Bridge.

UNITED SERVICE MUSEUM, SCOTLAND YARD, PARLIAMENT STREET.—By member's order.

WESTMINSTER ABBEY.—The vergers are in attendance from nine to six daily in summer, and from eleven to half-past two in winter (Sundays excepted). A small fee is chargeable to view the chapel and choir.

WESTMINSTER HALL.—Free during the whole of the day, or any hour at which Parliament or the law courts are sitting.

WINDSOR CASTLE.—Twenty-one miles from London by Great Western or South-Western Railway. The State apartments are open at intervals to the public gratuitously, on Mondays, Tuesdays, Thursdays, and Fridays. Tickets may be obtained of Messrs. Colnaghi, 14, Pall Mall East; Mr. Mitchell, 33, Old Bond Street; or Mr. Wright, 60, Pall Mall.

WOOLWICH ARSENAL, DOCKYARD, ETC.—Admission free to the Arsenal on Tuesdays and Fridays, by letter from the Under Secretary of War. Admission to the Dockyard every day, from nine till eleven, and from one till four.

INDEX.

A B C Railway Guide, special use of, 10.

Accident, imminent, how to act in, 102.

Across country place, anecdote respecting, 21.

———— places, best method of reaching, 131.

Address cards, necessity for carrying, 36.

Advice, letters of, to friends, hotel landlords, etc., 22.

After the journey, 121.

Air-cushion, convenience of, 74.

American railways, capacities and regulations of, 118.

Amusement, materials for, 75.

Anecdote about vehicles, 21.

———— of Captain B——, 39.

———— of Chuckley Slough, 109.

———— of family clock, 30.

———— of Lord B—— and Mr. G——, 79.

———— of Lord Guillamore, 103.

———— of the Rev. Mr. ——, 25.

———— of a season-ticket holder, 56.

———— of Sir Edward C——, 77.

Argument with travelling companions, caution respecting, 76.

Arrival at station, 41.

———— and departure, time of, to find in railway guide, 11.

Articles left at station, directions concerning, 128.

———— not immediately required, disposal of, 14.

———— required for immediate use, disposal of, 14.

Austrian railways, regulations and peculiarities of, 116.

BAGGAGE, collecting, at end of journey, 121.

Bags, travelling, various kinds of, 18.

Before the journey, 2.

Belgian railways, regulations, etc., of 116.

Boots for travelling, best kind of, 33.

Bradshaw's Railway Guide, how to read it, 11.

Branch lines, cautions respecting, 94.

Business travellers, hints for, 3.

Bye-laws and regulations, enumeration of, 112.

CAB, hints for choice of, 38.

———— engaging, at end of journey, 122.

—— taking number of, 126.

—— fares, adjustment and settlement of, 37.

Cap for travelling, best kind of, 32.

Card-playing as a railway recreation, 82.

Cards of address, best kind of, 16.

Carriage, choice of, 57.

———— changing, hints respecting, 90.

———— marking, for recognition, 89.

———— noting number and position of, 64.

———— truck to engage, 22.

Caution respecting entering and leaving carriage, 97.

———— against taking other people's luggage, 126.

———— against standing by door of carriage, 93.

———— respecting crossing the rails, 94.

———— on passing through tunnels, 93.

———— respecting the difference in clocks, 28.

———— against looking out of window of carriage, 93.

———— for cases of threatened accidents, 102.

Changing carriages, with a view of evading payment of proper fare, how punished, 114.

Chess-playing as a railway recreation, 82.
Children unaccompanied, to secure safe conduct for, 61.
Choice of carriage, 57.
——— of class, 52.
——— of route, 43.
——— of seat, 60.
——— of train, 45.
Class, choice of, in railway travelling, 52.
Clocks, difference in, to be guarded against, 28.
Comfort, materials for, 73.
Commercial travellers, information for, how obtainable, 4.
Companionship, economy of, 107.
Complaints of misconduct, 107.
Concussion, how to act in cases of, 104.
Conversation, as a recreation in travel 75.
Conveyance at terminus, to secure, 21.
——— to out-of-the-way stations, anecdote respecting, 37.
——— to station, hints respecting, 37.
——— to station, pre-engagement of, 23.
Correspondence, epistolary, the best method of providing for, 36.
Crossing the rails, caution respecting, 94.

DEFACING carriage, penalty for, 114.
Departure and arrival, time of, to find in railway guide, 11.
——— eve of, things to be done on, 23.
——— time of, fixing, 20.
Destination, arrival at, 21.
Direction labels, best kind of, 15.
Dogs, regulation concerning, 114.
Down-line and up-line, explanation of, 98.
Draughts in railway carriage, to avoid, 92.
Dressing-cases, various kinds of, 19.
Dutch railways, conspicuous features of, 116.

EARLY morning, to insure waking, 23.
——— rising, anecdote respecting, 25.
——— trains, to insure being in time for, 24.
Entering and leaving carriage, caution respecting, 97.
Equipage, travelling, hints respecting, 17.

Et ceteras, supply of, 34.
Eve of departure, things to be done on, 23.
Excursion tickets, advantages and disadvantages of, 48.
——— trains, travelling by, considered, 47.
Excursions, hints for choice of, 4.
Express trains, travelling by, considered, 45.
Eye-preservers, utility of, 74.

FAMILY clock, anecdote of, 30.
Fare, attempting to evade payment of, how punished, 113.
——— payment of, regulation concerning, 112.
Fares, rate of, by various classes considered, 54.
Fees to railway servants, regulation concerning, 114.
Feet, to rest commodiously, 74.
Females, unaccompanied, to secure safe conduct for, 61.
French railways, regulations and specialities of, 115.

GERMAN railways, regulations and peculiarities of, 115.
Government employés, hints for, respecting season-tickets, 8.
Guillamore, Lord, anecdote respecting, 103.

HAND-luggage, stowing away, 72.
Haversacks, convenience of, 19.
Health-seekers, hints for, 5.
Horse-box to engage, 22.
Hotel, choice of, 129.
Hotels, etc., information respecting 12.

INFORMATION from travelling companions, to obtain, 94.
Intimation of safe arrival, 126.
Intoxicated passengers, how to be treated, 113.
Invalids to secure railway accommodation for, 23.

JUNCTIONS, caution respecting, 94.

KNAPSACKS, convenience of, 19.

LADIES and children, disposal of, 123.
——— carriage, to engage, 22.

Ladies' disregard of punctuality, anecdote respecting, 29.
Lady travellers, to insure punctuality of, 29.
Letters of advice, 22.
Liability and non-liability of railway companies, 118.
Local information, how obtainable, 4.
Lodging accommodation, best method of securing, 22.
———————— hints respecting, 135.
Looking out of window of carriage, caution against, 93.
Luggage, care of, at station, 41.
———— careful disposal of, 73.
———— caution against taking other people's, 126.
———— classification of, 14.
———— cording, safest way of, 15.
———— direction of, best method, 15.
———— in excess, disposal of, 42.
———— labelling inside of, 16.
———— limit of, pointed out, 13.
———— list of articles to be attached to the packages, 14.
———— lost, to reclaim, 124.
———— quantities allowed specified, 42.
———— to secure on arrival at destination, 124.

MAIL-TRAIN, travelling by, considered, 46.
Main-line, course of, to trace in railway guide, 11.
Meeting friends at end of journey, 121.
Memorandum-book for the pocket, 35.
Messages, telegraphic, despatching, 127.
Money, small change, convenience of, 34.
Musing as a railway pastime, 83.

NAME of place, how to find, in railway guide, 11.
Night travelling considered, 20.
Notes, advisability of taking, 35.

OBSERVATION and inquiry, necessity of, 3.
Obstructing company's officers, penalty for, 114.
Omnibus conveyance to station, 38.
On the journey, 72.
Over-coat for travelling, best kind of, 33.

PACKAGES, exterior of, to preserve, 14.
Packing-up, directions for, 13.
Paper collars, etc., convenience of, 33.
Parcels forwarded by railway express, 130.
Parliamentary train, travelling by, considered, 46.
Pedestrians, best kind of travelling equipage for, 19.
Pleasure-seekers, hints for, 4.
Porter, hiring, hints for, 128.
Portmanteaus, different kinds of, 17.
Preliminary remarks, 1.
Preparation for the journey, 13.
Property unclaimed, what becomes of it, 125.
Punctuality, necessity of, 28.

RAILWAY acquaintance, etiquette respecting, 78.
———— guards, duties of, 106.
———— guides, observations on, 10.
———— insurance, explanation of, 49.
———— insurance ticket, disposal of, 51.
———— Passengers' Insurance Company, rate of premium, etc., 50.
———— privileges, examination of, 48.
———— reading, best method of, 82.
———————— choice of books, 81.
———— reading-lamp, best kind of, 81.
———— rug, comfort of, 73.
———— servants, treatment of, 105.
———— signals, explanation of, 99.
———— station, noticing position of, 130.
———— ticket, disposal and care of, 91.
———————— regulation concerning, 112.
———— travelling in excess, anecdote respecting, 6.
———— van for conveyance of luggage, 38.
Railways, American, capacity and regulations of, 118.
———— Austrian, regulations and peculiarities of, 116.
———— Belgian, regulations and peculiarities of, 116.
———— Dutch, regulations, etc., of 116.
———— French, regulations and special laws of, 115.
———— German, regulations, etc., of, 115.
Reading as a material for railway recreation, 80.

Recognition of strangers, mode of, 122.

Refreshment, best kind to partake of, 87.

———— how to obtain, 86.

———— previous to starting, advisability of, 88.

Return trains, noting time of departure of, 130.

Riding on roof, steps, etc., of carriage, law concerning, 114.

Route, choice of, 43.

SAFE arrival, sending instruction of, 127.

Season-ticket holders, class to travel by, 56.

———— hints for, 8.

Season-tickets, advantages of, 48.

Seat in railway carriage, choice of, 60.

———— etiquette of retaining, 63.

Seat, in passing train, to fix upon, 66.

Settling down for journey, 72.

Shunts to recognize in railway guide, 12.

Signalling guard in emergencies, 101.

Sir Charles Napier's idea of travelling equipment, 13.

Sleep, in railway travelling, best method of procuring, 84.

Smoking as a railway recreation, 83.

———— in railway carriages, law relating to, 113.

Standing against door of carriage, caution respecting, 93.

Starting, signal for, 70.

Station, looking out for, 91.

Station-masters, etc., information derivable from, 3.

Stopping stations, whiling away time at, 132.

TELEGRAMS, rates of, 133.

Telegraphic message, to despatch, 127.

Terminus, distance of, from place of residence or of business considered, 9.

Through-ticket, economy of, 48.

Ticket, ascertaining the correctness of, 70.

———— care of, 69.

———— caution against tampering with, 70.

———— instruction for procuring, 67.

Toilet requisites, portable receptacles for, 19.

Too late for the train, 31.

Train, choice of, considered, 45.

———— passing station, to ascertain in railway guide, 11.

———— stopping at station, to discover in railway guide, 11.

Travellers in general, hints for, 9.

Travelling bags, various kinds of, 18.

———— cap, best kind of, 74.

———— companions, securing seats for, 64.

———— hints respecting, 59.

———— unpleasant, treatment of, 108.

———— costume, best kind of, 32.

———— for ladies, 34.

———— equipage, various kinds of, 17.

———— parties, to insure comfort of, 60.

Trunk for family use, best kind of, 17.

Tunnels, passing through, caution respecting, 93.

UP line and down line, explanation of, 98.

VALUABLE effects, liability of railway company in connection with, 119.

Ventilation of railway carriage, to regulate, 92.

WALLETS, convenience of, 19.

THE END.